T0267089

Favorite Flies for the

GREAT SMOKY MOUNTAINS

Favorite Flies for the

GREAT SMOKY MOUNTAINS

50 ESSENTIAL PATTERNS FROM LOCAL EXPERTS

KEVIN HOWELL

STACKPOLE
BOOKS

Guilford, Connecticut
Blue Ridge Summit, Pennsylvania

To my wife, Mellissa,
thanks for the years of support and encouragement
and allowing me to chase my dreams.

STACKPOLE BOOKS

An imprint of Globe Pequot, the trade division of
The Rowman & Littlefield Publishing Group, Inc.
4501 Forbes Blvd., Ste. 200
Lanham, MD 20706
www.rowman.com

Distributed by NATIONAL BOOK NETWORK

British Library Cataloguing in Publication Information available

Library of Congress Cataloging-in-Publication Data available

ISBN 978-0-8117-7082-8 (hardcover)
ISBN 978-0-8117-7083-5 (electronic)

♾™ The paper used in this publication meets the minimum requirements
of American National Standard for Information Sciences—Permanence of
Paper for Printed Library Materials, ANSI/NISO Z39.48-1992.

CONTENTS

ACKNOWLEDGMENTS

Books are not an easy undertaking, especially one about fly tying. This book would not have been possible without the help of Jay Nichols and his team, who had faith that I was the right person to write the book and were willing to put up with my countless emails and questions.

Thanks to my wife, Mellissa, and office manager, Vanessa Rollins, for their hours of editing and proofreading to keep me from sounding like the crusty old fishing guide I am.

To my father, Don R. Howell, and uncle, Dwight G. Howell, for teaching me how to tie flies and my friends Lefty Kreh, Bob Clouser, John Brinkley, J. E. B. Hall, Walker Parrott, and Landon Lipke for their influence in my tying over the years. To Gonzalo Flego for teaching me the ways of tying from Argentina and that less material makes a more productive fly.

To my wonderful staff at Davidson River Outfitters, who kept the wheels on the bus while I worked on this manuscript. And all of my clients and friends I have fished with over the years, when it comes to a day on the water that I don't learn anything, it will be time to take up a new sport.

A very special thank-you to David Cannon of David Cannon Photography and Dr. Patrick Williams for the spectacular images they provided me for this book. Both have forgotten more about photography than I will probably ever know.

Thanks to Mellissa Howell, David Howell, Andrew Howell, Linda Michael, Zach Hart, Lindsay Rutland, Chris Johnson, Vanessa Rollins, Christy Voso, and all the others who tagged along on fishing trips with me and ended up becoming a photo model for the book.

But most of all, thanks to all of the people who fish and tie who have made books like this possible and have made it possible for me to make a living fishing and chasing my dreams around the world. There are very few fortunate enough to have made their passion in life their vocation. I consider myself very fortunate to be one of them.

INTRODUCTION

When you talk about the Smokies, most people assume that you are speaking about just the area inside Great Smoky Mountains National Park. However, the Smokies and the surrounding Balsam, Black, and Blue Ridge Mountain Ranges all feature the same geography, bottom structure, and small mountain plunge-pool fishing. So for this book I am going to refer to the Smokies as the general area ranging from Morganton, North Carolina, on the east to Elizabethton, Tennessee, to the north; Knoxville, Tennessee, to the west; and Helen, Georgia, to the south.

This is a rough and rugged area that is classified as a deciduous rain forest. The area features some of the most diverse ecosystems in the world, not to mention the highest peaks east of the Mississippi River. It was not until after World War II when drastic improvements were made to the infrastructure of the region that tourism and sportfishing started to take foot in the area. Up until this time, fishing was a means of sustenance to those who lived in the region.

The rugged nature of the Smokies and the Blue Ridge escarpment is what makes the area so good for trout fishing. The Blue Ridge escarpment drops some 3,500 feet in as little as a couple of miles in some places. The abrupt escarpment provides the orthographic lift that provides all of the

Like most of the streams in the Smokies, the upper Pigeon River features a high gradient and lots of broken pocketwater. All of this pocketwater makes for opportunistic trout. PHOTO DAVID CANNON

rainfall for the region. During the summer, thunderstorms are a daily event. Some storms get trapped by the mountains and end up dumping inches of rain on the head of a drainage in just a couple of hours. Winter and spring rains can last for a week at a time.

Due to the average 80-plus inches of rainfall annually, the region is brimming with streams and waterfalls. There are very few places in the world that offer as many miles of fishable water in as small of a geographic area as the Great Smoky Mountains. There are over 2,900 miles of streams inside the park boundary alone, with another 3,000 miles in the twenty-six surrounding counties of Western North Carolina, not to mention surrounding trout water in North Georgia and East Tennessee.

The combination of the high rainfall, steep rugged terrain, and deciduous rain forest climate makes the Smokies a unique fishery. The steep gradient and terrain create classic plunge-pool fishing for the majority of the streams in the Smokies. Every little hollow has a small spring or creek flowing out of it and into the larger creeks and rivers. The landscape is covered with waterfalls ranging from a couple of feet in height to over a hundred feet. Streams are lined for miles with rhododendron, mountain ivy, and dog hobble. All of this scenery mixes with crystal-clear water that requires anglers to have a super-stealthy approach, light tippets, and precision casts to avoid the ever-present overhanging rhododendron.

Massive sycamore trees also line the banks, with their pink roots running out into the clear water. It is here in the midst of these pink sycamore roots that anglers will encounter the prettiest brown trout they've ever seen as they take on a pinkish/orangish color from lying next to or in the sycamore

roots. In the spring anglers are greeted with brilliant green emerging leaves, blooming dogwoods and rhododendrons, and a multitude of wildflowers including lady's slippers, trilliums, and mayapples. Every fall brings a brilliant array of red, yellow, orange, and brown leaves mixed with the evergreen pines and rhododendrons. While the American West, Patagonia, New Zealand, and other regions are spectacular in their own right, the shadows, flora, moss-covered rocks, and clear flowing water of the Smokies combine to create one of the most spectacular settings for trout fishing in the world.

Fly fishing in the Great Smoky Mountains National Park region more than likely began when a forward-thinking Cherokee Indian tied a hook fashioned from a deer bone to his line. He then wrapped a brightly colored bird feather to the hook with a piece of rawhide and proceeded to dupe a fish into hitting it. From that point forward, fly fishing in the region was primarily for subsistence until late in the twentieth century.

In the 1840s Charles Lanman traveled the area, exploring the region that had recently been taken from the Cherokees when they were forcibly marched on the Trail of Tears from the Smokies to the Cherokee reservation in Oklahoma. Lanman, who traveled with a lancewood rod, wrote of fishing and camping with the remaining Cherokees and how they used flies to catch native specks (brook trout) and have them for dinner with corn bread that had been cooked with bear fat. Later travelers to the region, Charles Orvis and Mary Orvis Mayberry, wrote of encountering Cherokee Indians who dressed flies well.

However, most of the history of how fly fishing and fly tying began in the region will never be known. The culture of the Great

Smoky Mountains region was one of story-telling and song, and not much of anything was written down about the history of fly tying or fly fishing. Because of this culture, most of the fly tiers never wrote down how they dressed a particular fly. Over time patterns got changed, and patterns got lost.

We will never know exactly who invented some of the patterns or when and why they were created. It really was not until the park was established in 1934 that things began to be recorded in written form. Even then, fly patterns and how to tie them were closely guarded secrets from the outside world. It would not be until Fred and Arlene Hall, Dwight and Don Howell, Cato Holler, George "Cap" Wiese, Eddie George, and other mid-century fly tiers started to bring regional and national attention to the area that things would be widely recorded and efforts made to trace the history of fly patterns.

Both Don Kirk and Jim Cassada have made huge efforts to try to preserve the history and heritage of the southern fly tiers. The largest effort of all has come from Alen Baker, who brought his idea of a fly-fishing history museum of the area to life in the form of the Fly Fishing Museum of the Southern Appalachians (flyfishingmuseum .org). Dedicated to preserving the history and craftsmanship of the fly fishers of the southern Appalachians, and located on the edge of Great Smoky Mountains National Park, the museum is worth a visit.

The rugged environment of the Smokies, with its limited infrastructure, also provided little opportunity for tiers to gain access to commercially available fly-tying products. Tiers had to resort to using locally available furs and feathers or ordering materials by mail. My father and uncle ran a trapline before school every day to gain fur, and

Fall in the Smokies offers spectacular scenery along with some of the best fishing of the year. The one caution to fall fishing in the Smokies is that the major leaf drop usually occurs around Halloween, which can cause the rivers to be packed with leaves for a couple of days. PHOTO DR. PATRICK WILLIAMS

feathers were collected from grouse, turkeys, ducks, quail, and other game. Fred Hall, one of the first tiers in the region to achieve national recognition, supposedly ended up pawning one of his rifles to raise money to purchase fly-tying material via mail order. This inaccessibility caused fly patterns to get changed or modified slightly as materials would be substituted with similar materials. My father and uncle opened Dwight and Don's Custom Tackle in 1970, and along with Finkelstein's Outdoor in Asheville, was among the first in the region to offer commercially available fly-tying supplies.

I was fortunate to grow up under the fly-tying expertise of my father, Don R. Howell, and uncle, Dwight Howell. From 1970 until my father's passing in 1998, they, along with myself (as I got old enough), ran Dwight and Don's Custom Tackle Supply. They were world-renowned for their fine fly rods and custom-tied flies.

Some of the patterns in this book have four or five different dressings, and if you talk to any tier, the version they tie is the correct one. The versions featured in this book are the ones that were taught to me as a child growing up in the region by either my father or uncle or in some instances the tier who invented the pattern or their descendants. Other patterns like the Yallar Hammer have been altered because you cannot source the feathers of flickers, which like many birds are protected under the Migratory Bird Act. I have spent hundreds of hours dyeing different feathers to tie Yallar Hammers and have never found a way to reproduce a true flicker feather, which is a brilliant yellow on one side and iridescent black on the other. Another commonality of a lot of Smoky Mountain flies is the color yellow referred to in the area as "yallar." If you stopped in

any of the early shops of the region and asked what fly you should use, the common answer was anything with yallar in it.

Today Great Smoky Mountains National Park is the nation's most visited national park and the region is booming with tourism and fly shops. Tying classes are taught at most of the local shops, and most shops have some tying supplies. However, Little River Outfitters in Townsend, Tennessee, and Davidson River Outfitters in Pisgah Forest, North Carolina, feature the area's best selection of tying materials, and both shops have multiple nationally known fly tiers on staff to answer your questions.

Due to the popularity of the region and the fact that 65 percent of the nation can reach the area in a day's drive, I have chosen not to name a lot of the streams in the photographs in the book—not to keep everything secret, but rather I did not want to be responsible for concentrating hundreds of anglers on any one particular drainage. Instead, anglers exploring the region on their own will naturally be diversified and not concentrated on one stream, creating hot spots of pressured fish. Due to the extremely fragile ecosystem of the area and its biodiversity, anglers should only use maintained trails and paths so that we do not damage the ecosystem and create more sedimentation and water problems for the trout.

When Jay Nichols contacted me about writing this book, he told me to pick fifty flies for fishing the Great Smoky Mountains and to consider a mix of historically important flies, modern flies, and flies everyone should have in their box. My initial thought was, wow, that will be easy. The more I researched and started picking flies, however, the more difficult the task became. I wanted to expose tiers and anglers (especially those from outside the region) to some new patterns that they might have never heard of or seen, as well as some of the historical flies of the region. I knew from running a fly shop that the majority of customers coming through the door in the last few years are carrying Copper Johns, Hare's Ears, Prince Nymphs, Blue-Winged Olives, Mop Flies, and some of the other staple patterns that produce fish everywhere. I wrote my list out and started calling my friends and fellow guides who have fished the Smokies for years and asked them to give me their top ten list of flies. There were some patterns like the Parachute Adams, Inchworm, and Thunderhead that were on everyone's list, while other flies were only on a couple of lists. I took their lists and my list and compared and contrasted until I got down to fifty flies.

Some will question why a specific pattern is not in the book, like the Royal Wulff. I felt that it was commonplace enough that most anglers had already been exposed to the fly or had some in their box. Some flies like the Parachute Adams were ranked so high on everyone's list that I felt that they should be included because no angler should be in the Smokies without one. There are hundreds of flies that originated in the Smokies that did not make the book, again not because of a lack of ability to produce fish but rather because they are similar to other patterns already in the book or require materials that can no longer be sourced. I hope that you find the flies I have chosen to be interesting and worth the time to tie and try. I am confident that they will produce fish not only in the Smokies but across the country.

Higher-elevation streams in the Smokies feature a hard scoured-granite bottom structure, a result of the numerous thunderstorms and flash floods that occur at the heads of streams during the summer months. Due to the lack of silts and decaying wood matter, these high-elevation streams are nutrient poor and anglers will encounter opportunistic fish with large heads and skinny bodies. PHOTO DR. PATRICK WILLIAMS

Adams Variant
- **Hook:** #12-18 Daiichi 1170 or Mustad 94840
- **Thread:** Black 6/0 Veevus
- **Tail:** Golden pheasant tippet
- **Rear hackle:** Brown dry-fly hackle, slightly smaller than hook gap
- **Body:** Yellow ostrich herl
- **Front hackle:** Brown and grizzly dry-fly hackle, mixed
- **Wings:** Grizzly hackle tips

Adams Variant

The Adams Variant is often attributed to the late Fred Hall of Bryson City, North Carolina. However, it is a fairly common belief that Fred's wife Arlene, who was herself a world-renowned tier, actually created the fly. Regardless of which of the Halls created the fly, it follows all of the rules for a great Smoky Mountain fly—it contains yellow and floats exceptionally well in the swift waters commonly found in the park.

One of my early experiences with the Adams Variant was on Hazel Creek with my father. He and I had taken his boat across Fontana Reservoir to the Hazel Creek trailhead early one April. We walked just upstream of Proctor (a settlement prior to Fontana being built) and started fishing. It was a cloudy day, and a small hatch of March Browns was taking place. We were fishing along, and as the day progressed the hatch slowed and we would see an occasional spinner from the hatch the day before go fluttering by. The fish seemed to stop feeding on the March Browns and on top altogether. After several fly changes, my father put on an Adams Variant and seemed to start catching fish again. It could have been that they just started feeding again,

The Adams Variant is highly effective when mayflies with egg sacs are returning to the water to drop their eggs.

but to a ten-year-old boy it sure was impressive to catch fish on dries without any fish breaking the surface or signs of active feeding. I have long since come to understand that fish can easily be caught on top when they are not actively feeding if you present them with the correct fly.

I have always found the Adams Variant to fish the best from March through June when the mayflies are active. It seems that the pattern always fishes the best when a spinner fall has taken place or is currently taking place. It is also a great low-water dry fly because it is so light and lands gently on the stream without scaring the fish. Also, the materials it is constructed from create a silhouette but still allows light to pass through, making it less obtrusive to wary fish.

While named the Adams Variant, the pattern was an adaptation of an existing fly pattern called the Fore and Aft. The Adams Variant was created by adding a golden pheasant tippet tail, some wings, and a bright yellow midsection to the Fore and Aft pattern. The Adams Variant also features a grizzly hackle at the rear of the fly and a grizzly and brown hackle at the front of the fly.

While the Adams Variant is not an overly complicated pattern to tie, there are a couple of tricks that make the fly float correctly and fish a little more effectively. I have seen Variants tied with yellow chenille for the body, but a problem arises when the chenille absorbs water, causing the fly to sink. The original's yellow ostrich herl is the most productive and floats the best. When tying, fly tiers need to make sure that the grizzly hackle at the rear of the fly is one size, if not one and a half sizes, smaller than the front hackle. For example, if you are tying a size 14 Adams Variant, your rear grizzly hackle should be a size 16 or slightly smaller. This allows the fly to sit on the water with a three-point contact like a Catskills pattern. The other problem with larger hackle is that it will cover the hook point and make hooking a trout a more difficult task. I prefer to tie the Adams Variant with Light Cahill–colored thread; this way, any part of the hook that shows through still has a little hint of yellow to it.

Andrew Howell putting an Adams Variant to the test near Tom's Branch Falls on Deep Creek.

Overlooking the Hazel Creek Valley in the fall from US 441. Hazel Creek offers miles and miles of remote backcountry streams with camping at sanctioned National Park Service campsites. Anglers will need to make camping reservations in advance before starting a backcountry trek.

Backscratcher

- **Hook:** #10-16 Daiichi 1710 or Mustad 9671
- **Thread:** Red 6/0 Ultra Thread
- **Body:** Peacock herl
- **Rib:** Gold Ultra Wire (brassie)
- **Hackle:** Brown saddle hackle
- **Tail:** Brown biots
- **Wings:** Brown biots

Backscratcher

I was introduced to the Backscratcher by my grandfather in the early 1980s. He told me that it was an old Southern Mountain Pattern. It is believed to have been developed in the Avery County area of Western North Carolina, but there is no written background or history on the fly. If it did evolve in that region, I would guess that it was probably developed or at least influenced by the late Cato Hollar or George "Cap" Wiese, but this cannot be substantiated. Both of these men were close friends with my grandfather and father and influential fly tiers and innovators of the region.

I am not sure what the Backscratcher looks like to the fish other than a stonefly nymph or possibly a Woolly Worm, which are common in the Great Smoky Mountains as well as the high country of North Carolina. The Backscratcher was a favorite summertime nymph of my grandfather's. For the most part my grandfather was a dry-fly angler, and not just any dry fly but the bigger, the better. But when things would get tough, he would concede and tie on one of the three nymph patterns he had in his fly box.

One of my favorite fishing trips with the Backscratcher occurred on the North Toe River in Avery County. During one of my summer visits with my grandfather, we traveled from Spruce Pine to the town of

The Backscratcher works year-round, and most fish probably take it for a small stonefly nymph. However, lightly weighted versions fished in the fall will also dupe trout into thinking it is a Woolly Worm.

Linville and then down to the headwaters of the North Toe. We arrived to find the stream a dark tea color from the thunderstorm the evening prior. We tried all of his normal patterns—a Wulff, a Muddler Minnow skated as a dry fly, etc.—all with not much luck. So with reluctance he tied on a Backscratcher.

We fished the next pool and I caught a couple of trout on the Backscratcher but my grandfather did not, although he did have a couple of strikes. This pattern seemed to duplicate itself for the next few pools, and finally in frustration he ask how I was catching them and he was not. I stated that I was seeing the fish make my leader jump when they ate the fly. He grumbled something about his old eyes and scrounged around in his vest and produced a bottle of my grandmother's bright-red fingernail polish. I watched in confusion as he painted the knots of his leader with the red polish. As soon as it dried he went back to fishing as I watched in wonderment what was going on. Two casts later he was hooked up, then a few minutes later another trout.

So I asked him how the fingernail polish helped him. He said that with the knots painted bright red, he could now see the leader move when the fish struck the fly. He matched me fish for fish the rest of the day on the Backscratcher.

Over the years, I along with other tiers have tweaked the fly. Most of the ones I fish today, I have replaced the biot legs with brown rubber legs. The Backscratcher was so productive that it was the foundation for my father's fly called The Bug, which is without a doubt one of the best low-water summer nymphs I have ever fished. The Bug used both grizzly and brown hackle and gray rubber legs. The other main difference is that The Bug is very lightly weighted, usually only a few turns of .015 or .020 lead wire—just enough to break it through the surface tension and hold the line tight.

There are no real secrets to tying the Backscratcher other than securing the peacock herl body securely to the fly. I either wrap the herl through head cement or wind thread back through the body with black thread to help reinforce the body.

Christy Voso fishing near Bird Rock Falls. A Backscratcher is equally as effective in fast water as in the slower pools.

Bill's Provider

- **Hook:** #6-12 Daiichi 2220 4X-long streamer
- **Thread:** Chartreuse 140-denier Ultra Thread
- **Underbody:** Lead wire (.035)
- **Body:** 6–8 strands of peacock herl
- **Hackle:** Brown strung rooster saddle
- **Rib (optional):** Gold or black wire (x-small)
- **Legs:** Brown rubber (large)
- **Note:** Tiers should use a medium-size leg on #12 Bill's Provider. Tiers can also change the size of the lead wire to fish different depths of the water column.

Bill's Provider

Bill's Provider was introduced to my father in the mid-1980s by longtime family friend Bill Hale. Bill's favorite fly was the Bitch Creek Nymph, which he fished often. Bill knew that the large, flopping white legs of the Bitch Creek drew fish to the fly and resulted in more bites. The problem was when the water got clear the fish would refuse the Bitch Creek Nymph due to the large white legs. Bill started experimenting with different-colored rubber legs and bodies until he arrived at a very simple peacock body with brown hackle and large brown rubber legs.

Bill gave my father a few of his new creations as we were departing for a trip to southwestern Montana and told him, "Here, these will provide a few fish." My father tried Bill's new fly out on the Gallatin River, which was the first stop on our fourteen-day trip. By the end of our two days on the Gallatin, the fish had totally destroyed the half-dozen flies that Bill had given my father.

We returned home with a new confidence in Bill's new creation. I tied a few up and stuck them in my box for the next time I could get out on the river. My grandfather really enjoyed taking me fishing anytime he

The Bill's Provider is a great stonefly imitation. It is especially productive during times of high, clear water. Over the years, we have experimented with different body and leg materials, but the original pattern pictured here produces the best.

got the opportunity. So a couple of weeks after we returned to North Carolina from Montana, he came over to Brevard to spend a few days fishing the streams around the area with me. It seemed to be a much rainier summer than most, and the rivers were full and seemed to be slightly stained most of the summer. I told my grandfather I was going to try a new fly, and he kind of scoffed at the idea and tied on his tried-and-true Yellow Irresistible.

We fished the next five days around the park and the Blue Ridge Mountains, and I never tied on another pattern. By the end of the trip my grandfather had taken old trusty off and was a firm believer in Bill's new fly as well. For the next year anytime my father, uncle, grandfather, or I tried Bill's fly it never failed to produce. So my father gave it the name Bill's Provider because of its ability to always provide fish.

I have since fished this fly around the world and have found it to be effective in Argentina, Chile, New Zealand, and all over the United States and Canada. In large sizes it is just as effective for smallmouth bass as it is for trout.

When tying the Bill's Provider, tiers can do a couple of things to make the fly more

Author Kevin Howell releasing a brown trout that fell victim to a Bill's Provider.

High, clear water that occurs so frequently in the Smoky Mountains is an exceptional time to use a Bill's Provider. DAVID CANNON PHOTO

durable. I often add a rib counter-wrapped over the brown hackle, and for this I use extra-small gold or black wire. This makes the hackle more durable. To reinforce the peacock herl body, I coat my underbody of lead wire with fly tier's head cement and wrap the herl through the cement—this glues the peacock herl to the lead wire underbody and makes the fly almost bombproof. The original version did not have the rib or the cement under the peacock herl, and I have not found these two tweaks to make a difference to the fish. Tiers should also keep in mind that the hackle is a strung rooster saddle, not dry-fly-quality hackle; the fine barbs of the strung rooster swim and move in the current, whereas the stiffer dry-fly hackle is not as fluid in the water.

The Bill's Provider is just as effective in low water as high; however, tiers will have to adjust the amount of lead wire they use for the underbody based on the conditions that they are fishing. For most of the normal conditions around Great Smoky Mountains National Park, I use a size 8 or 10 fly with a full shank of .030 lead wire.

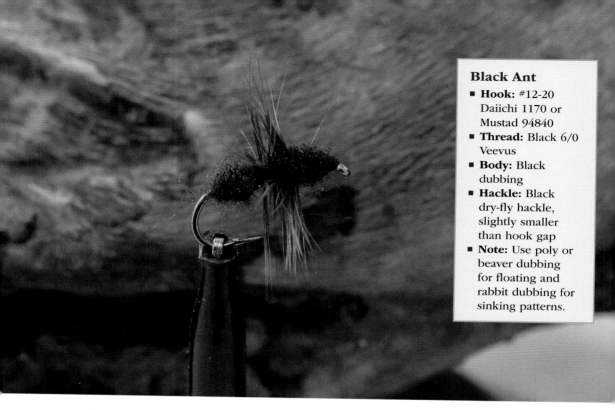

Black Ant
- **Hook:** #12-20 Daiichi 1170 or Mustad 94840
- **Thread:** Black 6/0 Veevus
- **Body:** Black dubbing
- **Hackle:** Black dry-fly hackle, slightly smaller than hook gap
- **Note:** Use poly or beaver dubbing for floating and rabbit dubbing for sinking patterns.

Black Ant

The Black Ant is often overlooked by fly fishers. Many anglers are looking for a flashier and glitterier fly to attract the trout. The truth is that ants are a viable source of food for trout in the Great Smoky Mountains region from mid-March through mid-November.

Ants are a particularly good fly to use in the early fall when the hatches are limited and the leaves are falling from the trees. You will often see trout eating the smaller leaves or swirling near a leaf then coming back to take a tiny morsel nearby. They are eating the leaf with the ant on it or knocking the ant off the leaf so they can come back and eat it. In the southern Appalachian Mountains we do not have swarms of flying ants like I have experienced in other parts of the world. We do, however, have large wood and carpenter ants that reach all the way from a size 18 to a size 12.

Most anglers tend to fish their ant patterns dry; however, in the Smokies any ant that falls into the stream does not float more than a few feet before the turbulent water pulls it under. Due to the turbulent waters, I tend to fish an ant with a glass bead or coated with Xink in order to turn the fly into more of a

A dubbed Black Ant is a must-have fly for the low, clear water commonly found in the Smokies during the late summer months.

Tom Dow's hot-spot foam-bodied ant that he used year-round.

nymph. The other thing I have learned over the years is that a lot of people fish ants to rising fish that are actually eating beetles. The best way to distinguish whether it is ants or beetles that the trout are feeding on is to watch the surroundings. If the trout are rising and there is no wind blowing, more than likely they are feeding on beetles that are flying and landing in the water. If it is windy, they are likely feeding on ants that are being blown out of the trees.

Over the years, I have caught plenty of fish on ants, but I had one client named Tom Dow who took fishing ants to a whole new level. Tom only fished Black Ants—rain, shine, snow, heat of summer, weather made no difference, he fished Black Ants. He would have me custom tie foam ants with a red dot on the head so he could see them for the spring and summer months, and fished a black-dubbed ant with a split shot in the winter. I had my doubts for a while that he was actually fishing only ants, but I would bump into him on the river a couple of times a month and that was the only fly he would have tied on. Tom always caught plenty of trout in the area streams and was always content to have one fly box in his vest.

Today there are literally dozens of variations of the Black Ant. Over the years, I have found a few of the variations to be as effective, if not more effective, than the original dubbed black fur ant. I have had the most success with a glass bead ant, which gives the fly just enough weight to punch through the film of the water and give the fly a little bit of flash. The key to tying a good glass ant is to use webby hen hackle for the legs to aid the fly in sinking.

I am also very fond of the Transparent, which sinks slowly and has a glassy shine. The original recipe called for black dry-fly hackle for the legs, but again I prefer a hen hackle. Quick-setting UV glue has made tying Transparents a lot easier, compared to the days when we had to mix epoxy and coat the thread to form the Transparent's shell over the thread. For times when the fish prefer a dry ant, I tend to lean on the Texas Piss Ant, which is referenced in this book.

Releasing a summertime brown trout that fell victim to a Black Ant. PHOTO MELLISSA HOWELL

Chubby Chernobyl (Royal)
- **Hook:** #10-16 Daiichi 1720 or Mustad 9672
- **Thread:** Black 6/0 Veevus
- **Tail:** Pearl Krystal Flash
- **Body:** Peacock Lite Brite dubbing with red Lite Brite center hot spot
- **Back:** Tan closed-cell foam (2mm)
- **Legs:** Sexi-Floss (brown)
- **Wing:** White floating poly yarn

Chubby Chernobyl

The first time I saw a Chernobyl Ant was in the late 1990s, shown to me by my good friend Park Burson. At that point in time, Park was the Hardy reels sales rep for the Southeast, and he and I would often opt for a sales meeting on the river instead of in the shop. Truthfully, that is probably why I bought so many Hardy reels back in those days. On the way to the river one early fall day, Park asked me if I had seen the Chernobyl Ant yet. He had seen and fished them at a sales meeting out west. I told him that I had not yet seen the fly, and when he showed it to me I immediately asked him if he thought we were going bluegill fishing. Park swore it was highly effective, but I still thought it looked far more like a bluegill pattern. We started up the North Fork of the French Broad that afternoon and it only took about thirty minutes before I was asking Park if he had any bluegill flies (Chernobyl Ants) that I could use.

The early versions of Chernobyl Ants were merely foam and rubber legs tied to a hook. Over the years, lots of creative tiers have added their own touch to the fly. The Chubby Chernobyl has been proven to be one of the most popular versions of the fly.

An almost unsinkable pattern, the Chubby Chernobyl (above fly tied by Montana Fly Company) is an excellent choice for those that like fishing a dry-dropper rig.

Chubby Chernobyls are great for rigging dry-dropper combinations, like the Chubby–Beadhead Stonefly combination being fished by Zach Hart.

Chubbys can be tied with any color of foam and in a wide range of sizes, and therefore can be used to replicate any insect from a large caddis to a stonefly to a grasshopper or other large land-born terrestrial.

The foam body and high-floating poly yarn wing make the fly almost unsinkable, which has led it to become the most commonly used dry-dropper fly among guides and anglers alike. These same characteristics also make it a great floating fly in the turbulent waters of Great Smoky Mountains National Park.

I have seen the Chubby tied in almost every color imaginable. Over the years, I have come to put most of my efforts into tan to represent a caddis, while black and other dark colors do well at representing beetles and stoneflies depending on fly size. Golden and yellow colors do the best for hoppers. Tied in a small size 16, a bright yellow Chubby will also work very well during the Yellow Sally hatches common throughout the summer in the Smokies.

When tying Chubby Chernobyls, tiers can cut their own foam bodies, especially for smaller sizes. I make a template from card stock of the desired size and shape and then trace it out and cut the bodies with razor scissors. Montana Fly Company makes a set of punches that really speed up the process of making bodies, but they are best suited for a size range of 8 to 12 hooks. While most Chubbys are tied on regular long-shank hooks, I prefer to tie my personal flies on a slightly curved hook like the Tiemco 200R. I feel that I get a little better hookup ratio with the hook point sitting a little lower in the water.

Zach Hart releases an eager brown trout that ate a Chubby Chernobyl.

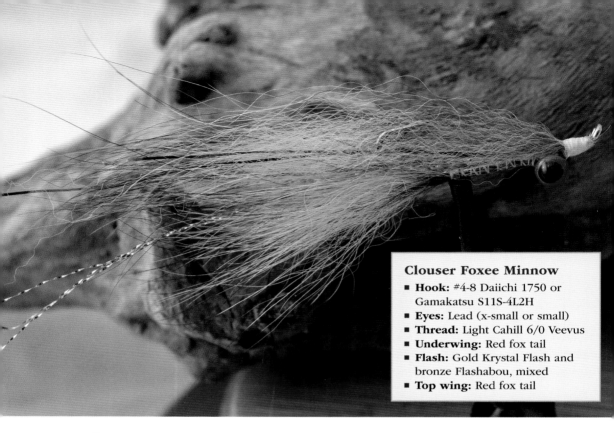

Clouser Foxee Minnow
- **Hook:** #4-8 Daiichi 1750 or Gamakatsu S11S-4L2H
- **Eyes:** Lead (x-small or small)
- **Thread:** Light Cahill 6/0 Veevus
- **Underwing:** Red fox tail
- **Flash:** Gold Krystal Flash and bronze Flashabou, mixed
- **Top wing:** Red fox tail

Clouser Foxee Minnow

The fly-fishing industry is a very small world, and you are never more than a couple introductions away from anyone you want to meet. With that said, I am not sure when or where I meet my good friend Bob Clouser—all I know is that he has been a friend and mentor for as long as I can remember. But I can for sure tell you the story of the first time he and I fished a Clouser Foxee Minnow. For many years Bob and I co-taught a fly-fishing school for the Episcopal Church, along with the help of my good friend Reverend Mark Wilson, at the Kanuga Conference Center just down the road from my shop. Bob would always add a couple of days to the trip, and he and I would spend those days fishing and swapping ideas on flies.

On one such fishing trip, Bob reached into his little bag of flies (literally a lunch-sized paper bag full of flies in plastic sleeves) he always carried and produced a Clouser Foxee Minnow. As I rowed, I watched Bob catch countless fish on his fly. After an hour

The Clouser Foxee Minnow is quite possibly the most versatile streamer an angler can have in their fly box. While designed for smallmouth bass fishing, this fly is my go-to streamer for trout anywhere in the world and especially in the Smokies, where we have a lot of tan-colored daces and darts.

or two of him just hammering on some fish, he reached up, clipped his fly off, and said, "Want to watch me catch even more fish?" So the challenge was on. Bob reached in and produced a second Clouser Foxee Minnow, same size and weight, but I noticed the fly was slightly different in color (it was a Blonde Foxee Minnow). What had been a lesson in streamer fishing became an outright obscene fish-catching gluttony of biblical proportion.

Since that time, I have used the Clouser Foxee Minnow in the original color and blonde variations from Alaska to Argentina. It is without a doubt my most universal streamer. Bob designed the Foxee Minnow for finicky smallmouth bass in clear water, but it has proven to be just as effective on trout as well as hundreds of other species from bluegill to bonefish. One of my good clients caught a 31-inch brown trout out of the Davidson River a few years back on a Foxee Minnow on a cold January morning.

The key to tying a good Foxee Minnow is starting with a quality red fox tail. It needs to be a fox tail harvested in the wintertime, as this provides longer, more supple fur on the fox's tail. Secondly, even if you get a very high-quality tail, you are still only going to be able to tie quality flies that swim correctly out of the bottom (part closest to the body) one-third of the tail. So many commercially tied Foxee Minnows are tied from the tip, or upper section, of the tail, and they simply do not swim well. Tiers need to be sure to remove all of the underfur from the long guard fibers, as the underfur will also prevent the fly from swimming well.

When choosing and tying in the flash, tiers need a combination of two strands of gold Krystal Flash folded over and three strands

Anglers floating the larger streams of the Great Smoky Mountains region will find that the Clouser Foxee Minnow is equally as effective on trout as it is on smallmouth bass.

of bronze Flashabou. If you use more than these few strands of flash, you overpower the fly and it does not seem to produce fish nearly as well. Also, allow your flash to stick about ¼ to ⅜ inch out of the back of the fly. When tying in the lead eyes, tie them one-third of the way down the hook shank from the eye to the bend of the hook. Most tiers have a tendency to place the eyes more forward, which will cause the fly to drop nose first in a jigging action instead of the gliding action achieved by the eyes being placed farther back.

For those that want to tie the Blonde Foxee Minnow, you will need to go to cosmetology class or at least buy some hair supplies. To achieve the blonde color you will take a red fox tail and use the same peroxide solution that women use to put highlights in their hair. I highly suggest that you practice this with part of an old tail before you ruin a perfectly good fox tail, because there is a learning curve.

Don's Pet
- **Hook:** Daiichi 1170 or Mustad 94840
- **Thread:** Black 6/0 Veevus
- **Tail:** Deer hair from back of eastern whitetail
- **Body:** Peacock herl
- **Rib:** Silver tinsel (x-small)
- **Wings:** Teal
- **Hackle:** Brown and grizzly dry-fly hackle, mixed

Don's Pet

Of all the large trout that I have seen caught, the catches by my uncle, Dwight G. Howell, on two consecutive nights on the Davidson River in May of 1985 with a Don's Pet are among the most memorable catches that I have ever seen or been a part of. Earlier that spring, my uncle had located a very large brown trout on the Davidson and spent countless hours fishing to it with no success. Late in May, with the Green Drakes hatching, my uncle approached the trout as my father tagged along with him. The large brown was rising and my uncle made a textbook presentation, only to be ignored by the trout. He allowed the fish to continue feeding while he changed flies. He tied on a Don's Pet and made another great presentation. The trout rose and sipped the fly in, and he landed the 25-inch beauty.

During those May hatches, my father, Uncle Dwight, his son-in-law Ricky Hubbard, and I fished every evening. The evening after my uncle's big catch, he and

Don's Pet was developed by my father, Don R. Howell. The fly was developed to be a dry-fly version of the Hot Creek Special, which has proven so effective in the low, clear summer waters of Great Smoky Mountains National Park. I, along with numerous other anglers, have also found it to be highly effective during the Green Drake hatch.

Intake at the Bobby Setzer Fish Hatchery, where so many large trout have been caught on a Don's Pet during the Green Drake hatch. Unfortunately today after several catastrophic flood events the Green Drakes are all but nonexistent in the Davidson.

Ricky were fishing the same stretch of water. When they reached the hole where he caught the big trout the evening before, my uncle turned to Ricky and jokingly said he was going to catch a larger trout. Dwight made a cast to a rising fish with the same Don's Pet he had been using the evening before. The fly settled, the fish rose, and then he realized that he had a very large trout hooked and had forgotten his net. So Ricky stripped his shirt off and crafted a makeshift net, and eventually scooped up Dwight's 27-inch brown trout into it.

In addition to being a big brown trout killer, Don's Pet is also an exceptional fly choice when chasing native brook trout in the Great Smoky Mountains. During the Green Drake hatch, I typically fish with a size 10 or 12 to match the larger-size drakes. The rest of the year I tend to lean more heavily on a size 16.

Over the years, my father and I have both played with the design and especially with the tinsel ribbing. I have tried everything from pearl to green to blue and always end up catching more and better fish when using the original silver tinsel. When tying Don's Pet, tiers need to size the tinsel to the size of the fly; on a size 16 I use an extra-small tinsel then switch to a small tinsel for a size 12. If you are having trouble sourcing the back hair from eastern whitetail, you can use groundhog (woodchuck) as a substitute for the tail material. Teal makes the best-looking wings, but tiers may substitute mallard flank for the wings if that is more accessible.

Female Adams
- **Hook:** #12-18 Daiichi 1170 or Mustad 94840
- **Thread:** Gray 6/0 Veevus
- **Tail:** Brown and grizzly hackle fibers
- **Egg sac:** Yellow Antron dubbing
- **Body:** Gray Antron dubbing
- **Wings:** Grizzly hackle tips
- **Hackle:** Brown and grizzly dry-fly hackle

Female Adams

The Female Adams is often credited to Fred Hall of Bryson City, North Carolina, located on the edge of Great Smoky Mountains National Park. However, most people that knew the Halls say that it was actually his wife, Arlene, who developed the pattern. Both Fred and Arlene were the first commercial fly tiers of the region.

The Female Adams is one of the flies that can be found in the box of every noted fly angler that fished in the park from the late 1940s to the present. It is likely that Arlene knew of the allure of the color yellow to the trout in the Great Smoky Mountains, so she took the already productive Adams and added some yellow to it. By adding the yellow to the rear of the body she also perfectly imitated a female mayfly that is returning to the river to drop its eggs. An egg-laying mayfly is in one of the most vulnerable stages that a mayfly will be in, and the bright yellow egg sac is like a flashing neon sign to the trout that are lying in the stream looking for an easy meal. Anglers will find that the Female Adams can draw some violent strikes; I am not sure why,

The Female Adams works best from late February through early May when the dark-colored mayflies like Quill Gordons and March Browns are hatching and the spinners with egg sacs are returning to the stream to drop their eggs.

but very seldom are the strikes a soft sipping motion.

I have found the Female Adams to be effective from March through July in the Great Smoky Mountains. From March through the end of May, the park experiences several mayfly hatches and every evening you will find various mayfly spinners returning to the stream to drop their eggs. During these times anglers can successfully fish a Female Adams at any point of the day, but the most success will be found from 4:00 p.m. on, until it gets so dark that you cannot see.

Moving more into the summer months, the Female Adams tends to work best at lower altitudes after a gentle rain when the streams have a pale tea color to them. However, some of the higher-elevation streams will have light sporadic hatches throughout the summer due to the water temps. Most of the high-elevation streams are somewhat acidic in nature or generally carry a low nutrient load, so the hatches you encounter on these streams will be very light, meaning you will see only a handful of insects. Due to the lack of nutrients and food in these higher-elevation streams, the fish will feed opportunistically on anything that looks like it could be food. However, those few mayflies are enough to make the high-elevation trout focus and feed on any passing mayfly, or in this case a Female Adams.

When tying the Female Adams, tiers need to be careful of the material they select to use as the egg sac. Over the years, I have seen them tied with ostrich herl, dubbing, yarn, and even yellow chenille. Chenille should not be used, as it will absorb water and cause the fly to sink in the turbulent waters of the park and surrounding areas. If you use ostrich herl, you will need to reinforce the herl with tying thread or drop a little glue on the hook prior to wrapping the herl on the hook. I prefer to use synthetic dubbing or just plain rabbit dubbing. If you use the rabbit, be sure to use a quality gel floatant on the fly when fishing it in the more turbulent waters. I do occasionally see a parachute version of the Female Adams, but that is the only variation that I have encountered.

High-elevation streams in the Smokies feature a hard bedrock bottom, very few nutrients, and little food for the trout. Because of the elements, trout in the high elevations are very opportunistic feeders. PHOTO DR. PATRICK WILLIAMS

Girdle Bug (Brown)

- **Hook:** #6-16 Daiichi 1720 or Mustad 9672
- **Thread:** Dark brown or black 70-denier Ultra Thread
- **Legs:** Flexi Floss
- **Body:** Brown chenille (medium)
- **Underbody:** Lead wire (.030 diameter)

Girdle Bug

The Girdle Bug (aka Pat's Rubber Legs) was developed by Frank McGinnis for use on Montana's Big Hole River sometime in the late 1930s to early 1940s and was originally called the McGinnis Ruggerlegs. It is a common belief among tiers that the fly got renamed the Girdle Bug over time due to the fact that a lot of tiers were taking women's girdles and dismantling them to get the strands of rubber for tying the fly's legs. For nearly ninety years the Girdle Bug has been imitating stoneflies and fooling fish around the world.

To be honest, I do not know how old I was when I tied or fished my first Girdle Bug. I do know that it was one of the first flies I was taught to tie by my father. From the time I was ten or twelve, I can remember many trips fishing with a Girdle Bug. For years I treated it as a high water, muddy water fly. In this scenario I caught a lot of large trout on the Girdle Bug, but it was not until I started guiding that I began to use the fly in clear water. Over the years, I have found that the Girdle Bug will produce fish for my clients day in and day out, and there is rarely a day on the water I don't fish one at some point. I have even found the Girdle Bug in larger sizes to be extremely effective on smallmouth bass as well. In general I like

The Brown Girdle Bug (aka Pat's Rubber Legs, Flexi Stonefly, or Ole Rubberlegs) is the single most used fly by the guides of the region. The rubber legs give the fly life, and it produces fish regardless of how bad an anger's drift may be.

Matching the hatch: A Girdle Bug is a perfect match for brown and black stoneflies.
PHOTO DAVID CANNON

to use a size 8 Girdle Bug tied on a 4X-long streamer hook, though I do tend to downsize for clear and low water. I will fish all the way down to a size 14 but put most of my faith in a size 10 as the low-water standard.

The Girdle Bug can be tied in countless colors: black, black and brown, purple, olive, olive and rust, peacock herl body, and countless other variations. To change the body color, simply use a medium chenille of the desired color. Tiers can use any color combination for the legs as well. A favorite for the Smokies is a black body with yellow rubber legs.

I tie my Girdle Bugs heavy to hold the bottom and stay in the zone with the real stoneflies. I prefer to use .030 to .055 lead wire and no bead on my Girdle Bugs, but when I tie with a bead I prefer a black tungsten bead.

The key to tying a really effective Girdle Bug is, of course, the rubber legs. I have found over the years that square rubber legs produce more movement than their round counterparts. I prefer the Living Rubber brand for tying legs on any nymph,

especially Girdle Bugs. If I cannot source the Living Rubber brand, then I prefer to use Spanflex or Flexi Floss, which are square or rectangular in nature and have a lot of movement. For muddy or high water, I like medium or large rubber legs, which create more motion and movement. For low-water and clear-water situations, I tie with small to medium legs. For body material I typically use a medium rayon chenille or variegated chenille. I also like to tie a peacock version, where I use five to eight strands of peacock herl. To increase the durability of the fly, I coat the lead underbody with fly head cement and wind the herl through the head cement, which will result in a super-tough and durable fly.

As with any fly that has been around for nearly a century, other versions have shown up over the years. Today you will see flies called Pat's Rubber Legs, Smoky Mountain Girdle Bug, and Beadhead Girdle Bug. Most of these variations are basically changes to the color of the body of the fly or the legs. I have found a lot of success fishing a jigged (tied on a jig hook with a tungsten bead) version of the Girdle Bug.

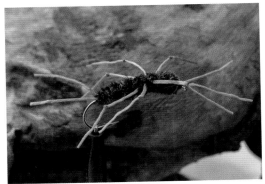

The Peacock Herl Girdle Bug (tied by Rio Flies) is a great choice for pressured fish, as the iridescent sheen of the peacock makes the fly look more lifelike.

Hot Creek Special
- **Hook:** #8-12 Daiichi 1550 or Mustad 3906
- **Thread:** Olive 6/0 Veevus
- **Tail:** Olive hackle fibers
- **Body:** Peacock herl
- **Legs:** Peacock herl
- **Back:** Turkey tail feather

Hot Creek Special

July and August can present some very challenging fishing for anglers in and around the Great Smoky Mountains. Some years you will be faced with low water or warm water, or sometimes both. In the low, ultra-clear water of the Smokies, trout become finicky and presentations have to be super delicate. Flies also have to be lightly weighted so as not to spook fish upon entry.

My father developed the Hot Creek Special for just such an occasion. As a kid, I would sit down in the tying room with him and take his scrap material and try to create my own flies on his old Herter's vise that

he tied on when he was a child. One day while he was tying Zug Bugs, I wound a bunch of peacock herl scraps on a hook and handed it over to him. He commented on how good it was and how he knew my grandfather would pay a quarter for that one. What my father did not tell me until years later was that the fly I gave him looked a lot like a Japanese beetle and that he had taken my creation and refined it into the Hot Creek Special.

While the Hot Creek Special is not a fly I would carry in my box every day of the year, it is one that I will not leave home

The Hot Creek Special is the ultimate summertime low-water nymph. With barely just enough weight to get the fly through the surface film, the Hot Creek is a great substitute for a floating beetle pattern.

without in the summer months. Fishing the Hot Creek Special requires a special presentation. The first adaptation to your gear is to lengthen your leader out to 11 to 12 feet in total length, the last 3 feet of which should taper to 6X tippet. Next, you will need to get rid of any strike indicator system that you are using and just go old-school and watch your leader and line for movement. To make this easier I take Mucilin and grease my fly line and leader all the way to the point where my tippet is tied in, usually the last 3 feet. By doing this your fly line and leader will sit high on the water, only allowing the last 3 feet to sink. If you see any movement in the leader or line, set the hook.

While I have fished the Hot Creek Special in just about every drainage in the Smokies, my fondest memory comes from fishing a small stream on the edge of the park which I will leave unnamed so as to not put more pressure on a small stream than it can handle. My buddy John Brinkley and I were out for a day of fishing and arrived at a place we called "the campground" (a large hole where everyone hangs out) and started fishing up the stream. I already had a Hot Creek tied on from a trip the day before. By the time I finished fishing the first pool, John had one tied on. To this day I am not sure if it was that good or if the fish were eating everything that day, but we were catching four to six fish out of every pool on the Hot Creek Specials that we were using. We got so wrapped up in our fishing that we fished to the base of a large waterfall that we had only been to a couple of times. We decided that the fishing was so good that we would just keep going, so we navigated around the falls in the woods and kept fishing and catching fish. By the time we found a way out to the road, it took us nearly two hours to walk the windy road back to where we had left the car.

When tying the Hot Creek Special, the hook should be very lightly weighted; I typically use .010 or .015 lead wire. You should use the lower, stiffer part of the peacock herl for the legs. Once they are tied in, I drop a little bit of head cement on them to help stiffen them at the base and make the fly a little more durable. Tiers should also leave a little bit of the turkey tail hanging out over the eye of the hook to form a head.

The Hot Creek Special excels in the low, clear summertime water around Great Smoky Mountains National Park. PHOTO DR. PATRICK WILLIAMS

Howell's Shuck It Jig

- **Hook:** #12-16 Gamakatsu J20
- **Bead:** Slotted black nickel tungsten
- **Body:** SLF Red Fox Squirrel Thorax Dubbing
- **Rib:** Pearl Flashabou
- **Thorax:** Blue dun UV Ice Dub
- **Collar:** Brown CDC

Howell's Shuck It Jig

I was finding so much success a while back with the early jig-style nymphs that I started experimenting with almost every fly idea I could. One of the best nymphs I had found during caddis activity was the Dirty Bird, with its dark dubbed soft-hackle-style collar and thin pupa-shaped body. So I started playing with the best way to get a fly like the Dirty Bird tied on a jig hook.

My early attempts at creating a fly similar to the Dirty Bird on a jig hook proved a little awkward with the angle of the head, hook shank differences, etc. One day on a trip with my buddy Bob Camenzind, we were walking in to fish a remote stream and I found a fly box lying on the ground—no name or anything on the box—and when I opened it I saw that most of the hooks had rusted. But whoever had lost the box had been a pretty creative tier. In the box was a Hare's Ear Nymph with a cul de canard (CDC) collar, and it dawned on me how much CDC moved in the water. Why not try that on my fly? I returned home and tied a few of the jig flies with a CDC collar and brought them to the shop.

Since I was spending more time in the shop than on the water during those days, I

Howell's Shuck It Jig is a cross between a European-style jig nymph and a soft hackle. The CDC collar gives the fly lots of life in the water, while the large tungsten bead keeps the fly down in the strike zone.

handed some out to the guides. Jeff Furman, one of the guides as well as a friend, took some and said he would give them a try. Jeff returned from his trip the following day and said he had never seen anything like it—that it was the only fly that had caught fish. The word spread quickly through the shop, and by the end of the week I was tying the little jig nymph for the majority of the guide staff.

Finally, in late September, I got the opportunity to do a little fishing myself and convinced my oldest son, David, to skip a couple of days of class and head to the stream with me. We arrived at our favorite stream to find the fish being a little picky; we caught a few fish on Zebra Midges and one or two on other flies here and there. Then I remembered the jig flies I had tied. I tied one on and caught a few fish, but again nothing special. The next morning I had the same rig still on and caught a fish on my first cast (which we all know is not necessarily a good thing). Two casts later I caught another brown trout. As the day went on, I was catching several trout to David's occasional fish.

Since then I have kept refining the fly. When I submitted the fly to my buddy Jake at Montana Fly Company, he told me he needed a name for it. I wish there was some cool story behind how it got its name, but all I could come up with was that the CDC made it look like it had a shuck. So I named it the Shuck It Jig.

I have found the Shuck It Jig to be a great nymph for imitating a caddis pupa/larva. It proved so effective that it was one of the first jig-style flies produced and promoted by Montana Fly Company. I often fish it in tandem with a Jig Pheasant Tail or a Trip Saver, and that is the rig I end up fishing all day. In addition to its effectiveness, it is super easy and quick to tie.

When tying a Shuck It Jig, I do not over-size the bead, like I do on some other jig-style flies. In addition, tiers need to use caution not to overburden the fly with CDC. I make no more than two full wraps of the CDC feather—more than that will cause the barbs to cling and stick together and the fly will have limited movement in the water.

David Howell tempting the trout in early October with a Shuck It Jig on one of our favorite streams.

Howell's Trip Saver

Howell's Trip Saver
- **Hook:** #10-16 Daiichi 1710 2X long
- **Bead:** Black nickel silver tungsten
- **Thread:** Black 6/0 Veevus
- **Legs:** Rubber (small)
- **Body:** SLF Red Fox Squirrel Abdomen Dubbing
- **Rib:** Pearl tinsel (small)
- **Hackle:** Partridge soft hackle
- **Collar:** Blue dun UV Ice Dub
- **Note:** Soft-hackle speckled hen's back can be substituted for the collar hackle. You can also use peacock Ice Dub for the collar. On the smaller sizes, I use extra-small rubber legs.

A lot of fly anglers are highly opposed to competitive trout fishing. Yes, there are a lot of downsides, but at the same time, competitive events cause us to experiment with different techniques, flies, rods, fly lines, and the list goes on. The Trip Saver is one of the flies that was born out of competitive fly fishing.

As a competitive angler, you are always looking for an edge or advantage over your fellow competitors. I am, by nature, a pretty competitive fellow and always want to have an edge if possible. During my years on the tournament circuit, I have done everything from cutting dog and kids' toys apart for tying material to taking a few snippets of hair from my neighbor's prize-winning Labradoodle. After a lifetime of fly fishing, you begin to understand fish and see patterns in what fish like. Here are some simple design principles: Any nymph is a good nymph as long as it has rubber legs, trout are attracted to peacock herl, and soft hackles will catch fish when all else fails.

As I sat at my tying desk pondering those ideas, I got to thinking, what if we could combine all of that into one fly? So the process began. The first version I called the

The Trip Saver is the fly I have used to win the Fly Fishing Masters and several other tournaments over the years. It can be fished as a stonefly nymph, or remove the legs and fish it as a caddis nymph.

Peacock Ear because of the use of peacock herl and hare's ear dubbing, then versions two to fifteen never even had names. This was all taking place about the same time as a fly called the Convertible was gaining popularity, so I thought, what if my fly could be adjusted on the stream without any tools or effort? The final version of the fly featured small rubber legs fore and aft that could easily be snapped off to create a smaller, more realistic profile if needed, along with a soft-hackle collar that could easily be altered to go from a soft-hackle-style fly to basic nymph in a matter of seconds.

For three years I carried the flies in a small plastic cup tucked deep in my vest so anyone that was prowling through my vest would have a difficult time finding them. The fly was super fishy and often allowed me to score a trout while fishing behind other anglers. This allowed me to present a fly that most trout had never seen before. Finally one day, on a nationally televised tournament, my good buddy Curtis Fleming called me out with those subtle words, "I have never seen a fly like that. What is it called, and how is it working today?" Just like that, with a TV camera stuck in my face, the secret was out.

Although I had been fishing the fly with my teammate and great friend Walker Parrott,

Caught by the camera rigging a Howell's Trip Saver. PHOTO DAVID CANNON

David Howell working a trout out of a logjam that he fooled by allowing a Trip Saver to drift back into the logjam and then twitching it back out.

who also guided for me at the shop, we both had sworn we would not tell anyone about it. So after a trip, Walker would come in and say, "Your fly saved the trip again today." So with the word out nationally and knowing how well it produced fish, I decided to name the fly the Trip Saver. I called up my friend Bruce Olson at Umpqua Feather Merchants and told him I was sending him my secret fly to produce. Bruce told me that I had missed the cutoff for the year and the fly would be held for a year before its release. But after receiving my samples, he called and informed me that Umpqua was going to have a rare mid-season release and that the Trip Saver was going to be the highlight of the release.

Over time, I changed the peacock herl collar to UV Ice Dub, which seemed to produce fish better than the original peacock herl and was far more durable. I have also explored other color options and have found a caddis green color to be effective during certain times of the year, but the original seems to produce fish year-round. While it does not realistically replicate any one food source for trout, this fly offers a very suggestive food form to the fish.

Humpy (Yellow)
- **Hook:** #10-18 Daiichi 1170 or Mustad 94840
- **Thread:** Bright yellow 6/0-8/0 Veevus
- **Tail:** Elk or moose hock
- **Wings:** Yearling elk
- **Body:** Bright yellow floss
- **Body shell:** Butt ends of wings
- **Hackle:** Brown and grizzly dry-fly hackle

Humpy

If there has ever been a better fly created to catch southern strain brook trout, I have never seen it. Not that a brookie is a discerning eater—as a matter of fact, they are pretty dumb and gullible and easily fall prey to gaudy, flashy objects. Which explains their fondness for a well-presented Humpy.

The Humpy began its life in the Hat Creek region of California as Horner's Deer Hair Fly, originated by the late Jack Horner. Pat Barnes would later come to call it a Goofus Bug due to clients walking into his West Yellowstone, Montana, fly shop and asking for that goofy deer hair fly. Jack Dennis would popularize the name Humpy.

When I first started traveling into the backcountry to fish for native southern strain brook trout, I fished with all the standard patterns like a Cahill, Adams, etc. On a trip with my grandfather, on some of the tributaries of the South Toe River at the base of Mount Mitchell, I would come to realize that there was only one brook trout fly. He showed up with one little fly box and some tippet, and I asked if he thought he had enough flies. He replied, "All I need." When he opened his box he had a few Humpies in different colors, all in a size 16, a couple of Wulffs, and a fly called Don's Pet that my father had created. He said, "If I can't catch

The Yellow Humpy has long been a favorite of Smoky Mountain anglers, especially those targeting native southern strain brook trout in the higher elevations.

them on these, then I guess they will stay in the river." As we fished up the small stream, the little brookies would all but rocket off the bottom of the crystal-clear pools to ingest the small size 16 Humpy. Even when you missed one, all you had to do was put the fly back in the small plunge pool and the brookies would make multiple attempts until they ate it.

Later in life, after learning more about insects and stream habitat, I quickly came to realize that the small-stream trout don't have the food sources that the larger rivers have. They are opportunistic in that if it looks interesting, they are going to check it out, and the only way a trout can check a bug out is to eat it, or at least try to eat it. To this day, my small-stream brook trout selection is a Yellow or Red Humpy. I have, on occasion, had great success with chartreuse, but it's not as predictable as the yellow and red colors. I also carry a couple of Wulffs or other bright, flashy dries, just like my grandfather, and have added a couple of

Brook trout have long been the prized fish of the Smokies. They are the only trout native to the region; the brown and rainbow trout were introduced after heavy logging had decimated the brook trout populations. Today native southern strain brook trout will be found above 3,500 feet in elevation and natural barriers like waterfalls that the browns and rainbows cannot get above.

shiny nymphs just in case I have to do some dry-dropper fishing. But 90 percent of the time I still rely solely on the Humpy.

The Humpy can be a complex pattern to tie and keep balanced and in correct proportions. Originally excess from the deer hair wings was pulled over to make the hair back (hump). Tiers then started using the excess of the tail to form the back of the fly, and in modern times I have even seen them tied with a brown or tan foam back, which makes the fly even more unsinkable. Tiers should find the method that best fits their style of tying. Don't be afraid to play around with various body colors; over the years, I have seen every color imaginable. I have had success with orange, chartreuse, black, and purple body colors in addition to the original red and yellow.

Author Kevin Howell fishing one of his favorite little brook trout streams in the Cataloochee Valley. PHOTO MELLISSA HOWELL

**Inchworm
(Furry Foam)**
- **Hook:** #8-14
  Daiichi 1720 or
  Mustad 37160
- **Thread:** Chartreuse
  6/0 Veevus
- **Body:** Chartreuse
  Furry Foam
- **Rib:** Gold wire
  or Chartreuse
  wire(brassie)

Inchworm

While it is not known who created the Inchworm pattern or when, the one undisputable fact is that every angler in the Appalachian Mountains should not leave home without this fly. There are literally hundreds of patterns that have been developed over the years to mimic the inchworm. Some of the most popular variations are the Green Weenie and the Mop Fly.

Every year from mid-May until the first heavy frost in October, the small green inchworms can be found hanging from little silk strings all through the Appalachian Mountains. These fluorescent little worms offer high protein and an easy meal to any trout or bass swimming along under the dense forest vegetation. As a guide, I have seen trout move as much as 25 feet to grab an inchworm that drops into the stream. While effective anytime during the summer months, the Inchworm pattern seems to be most effective right after a passing afternoon thunderstorm or rain shower. These rain events dislodge and knock the inchworms into the stream, and the trout definitely take notice.

Over the years, I have come to rely on the Furry Foam Inchworm the most. While trout will feed on an inchworm anywhere in the water column, they are especially fond

If you take nothing else away from this book, the Furry Foam Inchworm is the one fly that no angler should ever go fishing in the region without. Trout in the Smokies are so predisposed to eat Inchworms that we have caught fish on them year-round even when snow is on the ground.

of them when they plop into the water in slow-moving pools and slowly sink as they drift along in the current. I have found the Furry Foam version replicates this natural event the best with its slow-sinking action. Anglers can see the bright green Furry Foam Inchworms from a long distance off and will commonly see trout streaking toward their fly. Often this results in missed fish as anglers take the fly away from the hard-charging fish too soon. When fishing in faster, more broken water where the inchworm is going to get swept downstream quickly, I have found the Mop Fly or Green Weenie to be more effective, as they sink quicker.

Furry Foam Inchworm tied on a Mustad 37160 hook.

Beadhead Green Weenie. Anglers should keep a few Beadhead Green Weenies or Furry Foam Inchworms in their box—the additional weight will help get the fly down into the deeper pools and help hold the fly deeper in the water column when fishing higher water after a rain.

In smaller sizes the Inchworm pattern also represents the green rock worms (caddis larvae) commonly found throughout the region. This duel representation gives this fly a lot of credit in a fly box.

I prefer to fish Inchworms in a size 10 or 12 on a 9- to 11-foot leader tapered to a 6X tippet. If fishing immediately after a rain and the stream has a little color to it, I will drop back to a 5X tippet. The smaller-diameter tippet and longer leader allow the fly to drift more naturally in the slower currents. When switching over to the heavier Mop Flies and Green Weenies, you can fish 5X tippet and a regular 9-foot leader.

When tying the Furry Foam Inchworm pattern, tiers need to rib the fly or reinforce the Furry Foam so that it does not break apart on the first fish. For my personal use, I reinforce the Furry Foam by counter-wrapping a piece of small gold wire as a rib on the foam. When I am tying commercially, I use Light Cahill 6/0 thread and once I have tied the Furry Foam off, I wrap the thread back over the body to the bend of the hook then back to the front for the head and tie the fly off. I have not found the fish to make a fuss over which method is used, and both seem to secure the Furry Foam and give the body some segmentation. I also prefer to tie my personal Furry Foam Inchworms on an English-style bait hook like the Mustad 37160. This hook gives you an extremely high hookup percentage and causes the fly to fall a little more erratically in the current.

Both the Green Weenie and the Mop Fly are considerably more durable than the Furry Foam Inchworm, and tiers do not have to use as much caution in tying these two versions. Tiers may also want to add a brass or tungsten bead to the Mop Fly or Green Weenie.

From the time the leaves bud in the spring until the first heavy frost, every angler in the Great Smoky Mountains region should have an Inchworm pattern in their arsenal. PHOTO DAVID CANNON

Jack Cabe Hopper

Jack Cabe Hopper
- **Hook:** #10-16 Daiichi 1280 or Mustad 94831
- **Thread:** Black 6/0 Veevus
- **Tail:** Red hackle fibers
- **Body:** Dark brown mohair with sparsely mixed-in red and olive mohair strands
- **Wing:** Tan or ginger calf tail
- **Hackle:** Brown and grizzly dry-fly hackle
- **Note:** I prefer to use red calf tail for the tail, as the calf tail helps the fly float a little better.

The Jack Cabe Hopper is one of the flies that grew up in the Southeast and then migrated to other parts of the country. I was in my early teens when I met Jack for the first time. By the time I took over Davidson River Outfitters, Jack had owned Main Street Outfitters in Highlands, North Carolina, for a number of years. He was always willing to share some of his knowledge with me as a fellow shop owner and with any fly anglers that were willing to stop and listen.

Jack supposedly took inspiration from a fly out of the Michigan area to create his hopper pattern, which is more of a Trude-style fly than a true hopper. He developed the fly in the late '80s to early '90s, and it quickly gained a reputation for catching fish in the Highlands, Franklin, and Brevard areas of Western North Carolina. The fly seemed to work the best during the summer months and early fall and was found to be highly effective on those summer days when the trout were finicky. By the early 1990s, the fly was a mainstay in the box of every angler fishing in and around Great Smoky Mountains National Park.

The westward migration began in 1994, when Jack was fishing out west on the

While called a hopper, the Jack Cabe Hopper works best during times of stonefly emergence. The dark-colored body is a near-perfect match to the dark stoneflies found throughout the Smokies.

Stillwater River in Montana with Jack Yeager of Old West Outfitters. Supposedly, they were fishing together and Mr. Cabe was catching a lot of trout but Mr. Yeager was not having nearly as much success. Jack Yeager was so impressed by the fly that he started producing some Jack Cabe Hoppers to sell in his store. Over time the fly grew in popularity in Montana and today can be commonly found throughout the Stillwater and Big Hole River drainages, where it seems to consistently produce large trout, especially during tough conditions.

While the fly is called the Jack Cabe Hopper, it presents more of a stonefly profile to the fish than a hopper profile. I think most of the fish in and around Great Smoky Mountains National Park take the fly for the brown summer stoneflies that are common in and around the park after summer rainstorms.

Over the years, I have experimented with different-colored bodies and wings and have found that once you vary from the original pattern, the fly seems to be far less effective. I have determined that the body and the

Author Kevin Howell fishing hoppers under the overhanging rhododendrons and laurels in the Cataloochee Valley. PHOTO MELLISSA HOWELL

The large fields of the Cataloochee and Oconaluftee Valleys provide great hopper habitat, but anglers need to use caution, as they will also be full of elk.

wing are the two key elements to the Jack Cabe Hopper. The body should be thin and wispy and constructed from mohair yarn. The mohair tends to be coarse in nature and traps air bubbles as it sits on the water. The wing needs to be calf tail to help the long-shank hook float, especially with the mohair body. The wing is typically tied with a tan-colored calf tail, although the flies Jack gave me years ago had a wing more on the ginger side of tan than a true tan; however, that could have been the dye lot for the calf tail as much as anything. So I always try to stay with a tan to tan/ginger color for the wing. I seem to have better luck with the ones tied with red calf tail for the tail, but I have also used both red yarn and red Chinese saddle hackle barbs.

Over the years, I have fished the Jack Cabe Hopper in almost every possible size. I have found that sizes 8 and 10 are the most productive here in the Great Smoky Mountains region. I do occasionally fish a size 12, but only when the fish are swirling or swatting at the larger-size fly.

Jim Charley

- **Hook:** #10-18 Daiichi 1170 or Mustad 94840
- **Thread:** Bright yellow 6/0 UNI-Thread
- **Tail:** Medium ginger hackle fibers
- **Body:** Golden yellow floss
- **Wing:** Barred medium ginger hackle tips
- **Hackle:** Ginger dry-fly hackle
- **Note:** The original pattern called was tied out of golden yellow poly yarn; however, it makes bodies that look like something the cat puked up. I prefer to use golden yellow floss or thread instead.

Jim Charley

The Jim Charley is one the flies that just seem to have been dropped down on the earth. No one is exactly sure who originated the pattern, although most believe that it originated on the East or West Fork of the Pigeon River in Haywood County, North Carolina. Don Kirk makes reference in his writings that it may have been created by Charley Messer, but neither he nor I can substantiate those rumors. I can trace the fly back to the World War II era, which means it has survived some seventy-five years on the streams of Western North Carolina and East Tennessee in its original form. However, it is obvious in looking at the fly that is was designed to imitate the Yellow Mayflies (Yellow Drakes) and Sulphurs that are found in the region during May and June. In the early years, it was also likely fished to imitate the Yellow Stonefly.

I had heard of the Jim Charley most of my life but had never seen one in person until I was well into my late twenties and had just taken over Davidson River Outfitters. This always struck me as a little odd, since my father and uncle were known nationally for their fly-tying abilities and to my knowledge had never tied any Jim Charleys. As a shop

The Jim Charley is believed to have originated on the East Fork of the Pigeon River near Cruso, North Carolina. The fly is still popular on a regional level and is as effective as it ever was, but over the last few years has lost some of its allure as the older tiers and anglers have passed on.

owner, I would have clients come in and ask if I had a Jim Charley and I would reluctantly tell them no. It was Greg Frisbee, a longtime family friend and fishing companion, who first showed me a Jim Charley, which he had purchased from a tier over near Sunburst, North Carolina, where the fly is supposed to have originated. I told Greg that I was not overly impressed by the fly, which looked to me to be nothing more than a Yellow Mayfly that someone had mangled up with different-color hackle and a poly yarn body.

Greg and I went fishing that evening on the West Fork, where we knew there would be some Yellow Mayflies hatching that evening. I was fishing my standard Yellow Mayfly pattern and Greg was fishing the Jim Charley, and as we fished, the flies did not seem to make a difference in the beginning. However, as we got later and later into the evening, I noticed I would get an occasional refusal and Greg was not getting any refusals. Since that trip I have fished the Jim Charley side by side with the Yellow Mayfly several times and only had a couple of evenings when the fish seemed to prefer one over the other.

The Jim Charley has been so popular over the years that it has spawned several variations like the Jim Charley Royal, which features a golden pheasant tippet tail and small red thread section on the body just behind the hackle. I also believe that several other patterns like the Hazel Creek are a spin-off of the Jim Charley in that everything on the fly is the same except for the use of slightly darker hackle.

I typically fish the Jim Charley in sizes 12 to 16, with the size 14 being the one that gets the most work. Over the years, the bright-colored poly yarn has become increasingly difficult to source, so I make a lot of the bodies out of thread or floss these days and can't tell that the fish really seem to care. The fly is set apart from the Yellow Mayfly and Sulphur patterns by its trademark barred ginger wings and hackle. I have tried various ginger hackles on the Jim Charley over the years, but there is something special about the barred ginger hackle that seems to make the fish go nuts. I have even experimented with a parachute version of the fly, but did not find it any more productive than the original version.

The Jim Charley will provide anglers with some fast-paced action in late May. David Howell enjoys explosive dry-fly takes on the East Fork of the Pigeon River, home of the Jim Charley.

Kevin's Caterpillar

- **Hook:** #10-12 Daiichi 1270
- **Thread:** Black 6/0 Veevus
- **Body:** 5–8 strands of peacock herl
- **Hackle:** Golden straw Whiting Dry Fly Hackle
- **Antennae:** 4 strands of peacock herl
- **Note:** If tiers want to create a Caterpillar that floats well, they can build an underbody out of closed-cell foam. To create various colors, tiers need only to change the color of the hackle.

Kevin's Caterpillar

Kevin's Caterpillar was a fly born out of simple observation. In the early fall of 1996, I was busy building my house and one day while working on the roof I noticed that there were thousands of caterpillars (aka bagworms) crawling all over it. I reasoned that if there were that many bagworms on my roof that they had to be falling into the rivers as well. So when I got back home, I sat down at my tying desk and started to work on a pattern that would replicate the bagworms on the roof. Keep in mind these little guys pack the sting of a really pissed-off yellow jacket, so collecting a sample to go by was not an easy undertaking. Despite this obstacle, I managed to get three pretty decent replicas conjured up.

The next day my good friend John Brinkley and I headed to the South Toe River. We fished most of the morning and had only caught a couple of small trout. As we were nearing where we had parked, we had decided that since it was midday and the fishing was slow, we would just leave and move to a different stream. I told John before we left that I wanted to make a few

Kevin's Caterpillar is a fly that has a very specific place and time in the fly fisher's arsenal. It will outperform most terrestrial patterns in the months of August and September when the bagworms are most active, and it fishes equally well as a dry fly or as a nymph.

casts with the new fly I tied the night before. So I clipped off my nymph and tied on the Caterpillar pattern. On the second cast a nice 12-inch rainbow sipped the fly off the surface, much to my surprise. A few casts later, a second trout. John and I proceeded to fish the Caterpillars the rest of the day, eventually losing two of the flies and at one point climbing a tree to retrieve the third fly so we could keep fishing.

For the next couple of weeks, I kept tweaking the design, trying to make it more durable and better. Over the years, I have settled on two versions of the fly. On the dry version I add a small clump of black closed-cell foam to the hook shank before tying the fly, thus making it more buoyant. For the other version I tie straight to the hook shank; this version can be fished submerged just under the film or setting very low in the surface film, which looks more natural.

To make the Caterpillar more durable, I coat the hook shank with head cement before palmering the peacock herl down the shank; this glues the peacock herl to the hook or closed-cell foam so that the trout's prickly teeth don't ruin your fly after four

Releasing a brown trout that fell for a Kevin's Caterpillar. PHOTO DAVID CANNON

or five fish. Tiers will also find it helpful to drop a small amount of head cement onto the base of both sets of antennae. Tiers should use one size smaller hackle on the fly, so on a size 12 I will use a size 14 hackle, for example. Once the fly is finished, use scissors to clip the hackle barbs from the bottom of the fly. The hackle on the bottom of the fly should be just slightly longer than the peacock herl, giving the fly a yellow-over-peacock look without longer hackles.

Kevin's Caterpillar is best in the late summer and early fall. I usually start fishing this fly in late July and use it all the way through until the first heavy frost of the fall. August and September are the two prime months to use this fly. I typically tie it in sizes 10 and 12 for trout. In larger sizes, 6 and 8, I have found it to be effective on the smallmouth bass of the region as well.

Christy Voso works upstream in the early fall with a Kevin's Caterpillar in search of wild brown trout.

Kevin's Clipped Caddis
- **Hook:** #12-18 Daiichi 1170 or Mustad 94840
- **Thread:** 6/0 Veevus, gray to match body
- **Body:** Adams gray poly dubbing
- **Body hackle:** Grizzly dry-fly hackle, clipped to be no longer than ⅛ inch beyond body
- **Wing:** Dark elk
- **Hackle:** Grizzly and brown dry-fly hackle, mixed

Kevin's Clipped Caddis

One thing there is no shortage of are variations of caddisflies created by tiers in and around Great Smoky Mountains National Park. In researching this book, I found no less than five variations of the Woodchuck Caddis. All were tied the same, with just a slightly different-colored body. Even Kevin's Clipped Caddis is a descendant of the simple Woodchuck Caddis.

I started playing with the design of the fly when I was seventeen. I was headed west with my father, grandfather, uncle Dwight Howell, and our longtime family friend Herman Dellinger. We arrived at Herman's house in Ennis, Montana, in the early afternoon; I was eager to get in the water and within an hour found myself fishing the Madison River. Just before dark we got into a caddis hatch and I caught several trout on my first version of this fly. But I still felt that the design was not perfect, as some fish would refuse the offering.

I returned to the Southeast and kept tinkering with my fly. I swapped the woodchuck wing out for a better-floating dark elk hair wing. Next I wanted the body to have a mottled look like a true caddisfly, so I came up with wrapping a grizzly hackle over the

Designed to float in more-turbulent water, the Clipped Caddis floats well while providing a more realistic-looking profile to the fish.

body. I then clipped the barbs of the hackle down until they were long enough to provide the mottled look but did not affect how the fly sat on the water.

I started fishing the fly on streams around the area and kept refining the pattern. It was probably not until 1988 that the fly evolved into its current form. I found the approval (from the trout) that I had been looking for while fishing Cataloochee Creek. The Cataloochee can be a tough stream to fish, especially in the fall when the water is low and the fish are super spooky. I was fishing Kevin's Clipped Caddis on a long, 11-foot leader to keep from spooking the fish. There was a light hatch of October Caddis coming off. I had caught plenty of fish but still felt that the fly had more to offer, as I was only tying it in gray.

On the ride home, it dawned on me to change the body and mottling colors. All I had to do was change the grizzly hackle to a grizzly dyed whatever color I wanted the body to be. So I scrounged around in the tying materials and found a grizzly dyed orange hackle and produced a Clipped Caddis with an orange body with orange grizzly mottling on it and an orange and grizzly hackle. A few days later, I went back to the Cataloochee and gave the new fly a try. According to my fishing logs, I never had a single fish refuse the new color. Today I produce the Clipped Caddis in gray, October Caddis (ginger), yellow, and lime green. I use both the lime green and the yellow as substitutes for the Little Yellow or Little Green Stoneflies you commonly find around the park.

Tiers can choose any color poly dubbing to tie color combinations, though yellow, tan, ginger, and lime green are the most common. The other change on the variants

Yellow Kevin's Clipped Caddis. This fly also works well as a Yellow Sally imitation.

is to match the front hackle with the body color; for example, on the yellow I use a front hackle of grizzly and golden straw, and on the October Caddis color I use a front hackle of medium ginger and grizzly. On the lighter-colored color variations, I use a light-colored yearling elk hair. I carry various colors in my fly box in sizes 12 to 18. I rely on size 12 and 14 in the yellow and lime, size 14 to 18 in the gray, and size 10 to 16 in the ginger color. I have found that the trout will take the October Caddis version for a Tan Caddis, so I typically do not carry any tan ones and just substitute the October version for the tan when needed.

There are two keys to tying the Clipped Caddis. First, the hackle on the body of the fly should be clipped to be no more than $\frac{1}{8}$ inch in length and no less than $\frac{1}{16}$ inch from the body. This gives the fly the mottled look without affecting the way it floats. Secondly, the hackle should be smaller than normal—no wider than the gap of the hook. Tiers should also use a grizzly hackle in combination with whatever color hackle the body has.

Linda Michael enjoying an October Caddis hatch on the Davidson River.

Kevin's Stonefly
- **Hook:** Daiichi 2220 or equal size 6-12
- **Thread:** Black 6/0 Veevus
- **Tail:** Brown goose biots
- **Underbody:** Lead wire (.035)
- **Abdomen:** Peacock herl
- **Thorax:** White chenille (medium)
- **Hackle:** Large, webby grizzly hackle
- **Shell back/wing case:** Turkey tail
- **Rib:** Gold Ultra Wire (medium)
- **Legs:** Brown goose biot

Kevin's Stonefly

I started tying flies with my father around the age of six, and by age ten I was selling my flies to my grandfather for a quarter apiece. Let's be honest, I never saw him fish one of them, but it sure kept me interested in tying, and supplied revenue for my fishing addiction. By the time I reached age thirteen, I was tying professionally for my father and uncle's custom fly business.

From an early age, I was never one to leave well enough alone and was always tinkering with new designs and theories and looking for the next great fly. In 1985 I was on a quest for a stonefly nymph for the southern Appalachian Mountains that was more suitable than the big, gaudy stones from the western states that were available or being talked about. Taking inspiration and ideas from the Brooks' Stonefly and Montana Stonefly and my knowledge of how much fish liked peacock herl and its natural iridescence, I came up with the Kevin's Stonefly.

I tied up a couple dozen of them and set them aside for the next time I went fishing. Being a commercial fly tier means you work a lot during the peak of the season. With orders pouring in from around the country,

The original Kevin's Stonefly fishes the best when it is heavily weighted and on or near the bottom of the stream. If I had to choose one stonefly pattern to fish with the rest of my life in the Smokies, this would be my choice.

Kevin's Black Stonefly works best in the winter months when the little black winter stoneflies are active.

Kevin's Stonefly, rubber leg version

we were busy tying large orders of flies for both wholesale and retail customers. One of our local shops was running low on flies and begging for anything we could bring them. So in an unprecedented move, my father and I loaded up the two dozen Kevin's Stoneflies along with a little bit of other back stock we had and dropped them off. Never before had we sold a fly we had not fished. Less than a week later, the local store was calling begging for more of the stoneflies and telling us of the big catches the fly had been responsible for.

Once the season slowed and we had an opportunity to go fishing, we quickly realized that I had created an amazing little stonefly nymph that oftentimes produces trout when few other flies are working. I had created the original version with brown goose biots but less than a year later realized that brown rubber legs made the fly even more effective than the original version. While the original pattern with biot legs catches fish, the substitution of rubber legs produces a fly that is almost undefeatable.

I have made other tweaks and minor adjustments to the fly over the years, but for the most part it remains the same as it did in the mid-1980s. Kevin's Stonefly is best tied on a 4X-long streamer hook. The fly should be heavily weighted; I typically use a full shank of .030 to .050 lead wire. The hackle on the front of the fly is an oversized webby grizzly rooster feather, which after being tied in is clipped so that the barbs are even to the gap of the hook. This results in making the hackle a little stiffer and causes the fly to push or displace more water. Also when tying the fly, be sure the hackle on the sides of the thorax are cut on an angle that is closest to the chenille at the front and longest at the back of the thorax, thus allowing the rubber legs or biots to lie back along the side of the body.

If tiers are using rubber legs, I highly recommend square or rectangular legs, as they tend to have more movement and life in the water than their round counterparts. For size 6 and 8 flies, I use a large brown square rubber leg; for smaller flies, I use a medium rubber leg. For a more durable fly, I spray the turkey tail with clear Krylon spray paint and then place a drop of head cement on top of the wing case for added strength.

I typically tie the Kevin's Stonefly in sizes 6 to 12 on a 4X-long streamer hook. My favorite size to fish is a size 8. Over the years, I created a smaller black version to imitate the little winter black stoneflies found in the southern Appalachian Mountains.

Nymphing with a Kevin's Stonefly after a light rain, one of the author's favorite methods for the Smokies.

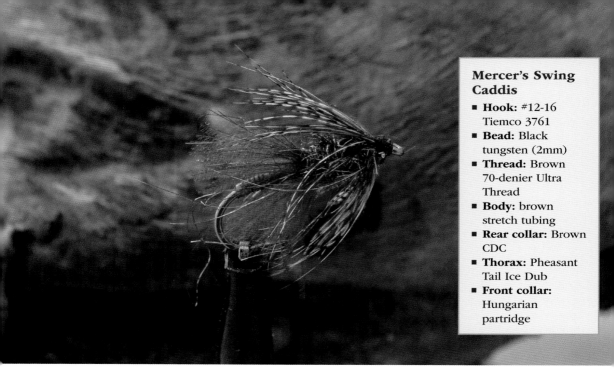

Mercer's Swing Caddis
- **Hook:** #12-16 Tiemco 3761
- **Bead:** Black tungsten (2mm)
- **Thread:** Brown 70-denier Ultra Thread
- **Body:** brown stretch tubing
- **Rear collar:** Brown CDC
- **Thorax:** Pheasant Tail Ice Dub
- **Front collar:** Hungarian partridge

Mercer's Swing Caddis

The streams in the Smokies, like most other streams in the United States, have lots of caddisflies in them. The importance of caddisflies in the diet of trout around the park can be observed by patterns like the Stickbait, which has long been a staple of anglers in the region. Mike Mercer's Swing Caddis has proven just as effective in the southern Appalachian Mountains and Great Smoky Mountains National Park as in the streams in the West. The Swing Caddis was designed to be fished as a caddis pupa imitation on the swing.

For years we fished a soft hackle on the swing as a caddis pupa imitation. When Mercer's Swing Caddis came along, it did not take long at all for the fly to catch on. With the addition of a tungsten bead the fly stayed deeper in the water column as it swung across the current, which seemed to result in more strikes and slightly larger fish.

On a trip to the Smokies with my friend John Brinkley, we were camping over on the Tennessee side in Cades Cove with our wives and fishing around the area. John and I had gotten up before the girls and ventured out to the Little River. As we fished, we were seeing caddis hatching; we went through our normal flies, and nothing seemed to work. I finally opened my box and saw a couple of Swing Caddises and started swinging them. I caught a fish occasionally,

Mercer's Swing Caddis works effectively as both a swinging-style soft-hackle nymph and a dead-drifted nymph. It is a favored fly of a lot of the guides in the region, as it can serve a dual role in the fly box.

but still nothing worth writing about. Perplexed, we kept fishing as we approached a larger pool of water where we noticed a very large trout taking caddis at the back of the pool. John rerigged and threw a dry fly to the rising fish, and I watched as the fish repeatedly refused his offerings.

John finally gave up and told me to give it a try. I said, "Watch this—I'm going to scare the fish and then we can go meet up with the girls," since it was getting late in the day. I made an upstream cast to the fish, and no sooner did the Swing Caddis start to drift toward the trout than he charged the fly and engulfed it. After I landed the fish, we stood there and decided it was time to meet up with the girls before we got in trouble with them. As we prepared to leave, I made a cast up into the pool to clear my line and wind it up on my reel. By the time my line came tight to my reel, I was hooked up to another fish. After I landed the second trout I told John let's try this again, and again the fly landed, started to drift, and a fish took it almost immediately. We ended up getting back to the campsite very late in the afternoon, and we were in the proverbial doghouse too. For whatever reason, the fish wanted the Swing Caddis dead drifted that day.

Since then I have fished the Swing Caddis both dead drifted and swung, and both methods produce trout equally well. I often use the Swing Caddis as a dropper on a heavier nymph and have clients dead drift the nymphs through a pool and allow them to swing out at the end of the drift before recasting. This method will produce a lot of fish that get overlooked—John has found it so effective that he fishes most of his nymphs this way and lightly sets the hook at the end of every swing out. This little hook set has produced countless fish that neither he nor I knew had struck the fly.

When tying the Mercer's Swing Caddis, most tiers tend to run out of room and end up crowding the hook eye, so be sure to leave more space than you think may be required. I like to tie with a couple different weights of beads to allow me to fish the fly in different parts of the water column. As for variations, I have tried different colors over the years. After a lot of experimentation, I have found the original brown and olive to be the two best colors.

Mercer's Swing Caddis has proven as effective dead drifted under an indicator as on the swing. Christy Voso dead drifts a Girdle Bug, with a Swing Caddis dropper.

Mike's Magic Beetle

- **Hook:** #8-14 Gamakatsu 921
- **Bead:** Green glass (3mm) Tyers Brand glass beads
- **Thread:** Black 6/0 UNI-Thread
- **Outer shell:** Mallard (#850) Kreinik Ribbon (⅛ inch)
- **Shell:** Black closed-cell foam (⅛ inch), cut to width of hook gap
- **Body:** 4–5 strands of peacock herl
- **Indicator:** Orange or yellow closed-cell foam (¹⁄₁₆ inch)
- **Legs:** Black round rubber (medium)

Mike's Magic Beetle

If you look at any fly catalog in the country, you will find countless beetle patterns. While they may all look alike on the surface, it does not take an angler long fishing with one of Mike Adams's beetles to realize that there is something magical about his patterns. Mike ties his beetle so that the fly lands right side up on every cast regardless of the caster's ability. Mike's Magic Beetle is a staple for southern Appalachian fly anglers from the Great Smoky Mountains to the tailwaters of East Tennessee from late June to the first frost.

While gathering information about the Magic Beetle for this book, I called my friend Mike and asked him about the fly. Anglers and regional shops often order Mike's beetles by the dozens, months and months ahead of time. While talking with Mike, he told the story of how Lefty Kreh used to come down and fish on the South Holston with him and would always remind him to bring some extra Magic Beetles so he could take some "to Tom." After several years, Lefty revealed to Mike that he was taking the Magic Beetles to his friend Tom Brokaw.

Mike spent several years guiding the South Holston and Watauga Rivers in East Tennessee. Over time these rivers became more and more pressured, and as guides

Mike's Magic Beetle (tied by Mike Adams). One of the most frustrating phenomena in fly fishing, especially with terrestrials, is that 50 percent of the time the fly lands upside down on the water. Mike's Magic Beetle will land hook down on every cast, greatly increasing an angler's productivity.

Bottom view of Mike's Magic Beetle, highlighting the bead. The bead is what makes the fly land hook down with every presentation.

and anglers we were always looking for new patterns and techniques to fool the pressured fish. Mike had a reputation for being the best guide on the river and always able to catch fish when others were struggling. I don't remember when or where Mike first gave me one of his beetles, though I would image it was at the takeout on the Watauga where we used to stand and talk after trips. I do remember how impressed I was that the beetle landed hook down on every single cast. This means you get in far more fishing time, as you never have a cast that results in the beetle upside down on the water, which results in more fish caught.

I have gained so much confidence in Mike's fly that over the years I have pared my fly box down to two beetle patterns, the Loco Beetle and Mike's Magic Beetle. I have even taken to tying my Loco Beetles in the same fashion as Mike's Magic Beetle so that they land hook down on every cast. After seeing how well Mike's fly performed on the tailwaters, I quickly started using the pattern in other freestone streams around the Smokies and found just as much success. Mike's fly has been so successful in the Smokies that the guys at Little River

Outfitters in Townsend say that it is one of their top-selling flies. Today Mike makes a living guiding on the tailwaters and tying beetles for several shops and a lot of his former clients.

After a lot of trial and error, Mike learned that sliding a small bead on the hook before tying the fly will keep the fly from landing incorrectly. The added weight of the bead on the underside of the hook causes the beetle to land hook point down every cast. In addition to landing correctly, the bead causes the fly to sit a little lower in the water, making it a little more desirable to the trout.

The only variations that I have encountered to the Magic Beetle have been derived by changing the peacock body to small estaz or changing the size of the fly. I primarily fish a size 10 or 12 the majority of the time, though I have on occasion employed a size 14 for trout. I have also experimented with tying the fly in larger size 6 or 8 and have found it will produce smallmouth in the larger sizes, as well as being a good trout size in the West and in Patagonia, where larger land-born beetles are present.

The abundance of lush green foliage in the summer months provides excellent habitat for beetles. Anglers will find beetles active in the region from May through early October.

Palmer

There are several theories as to where and how the Palmer originated. It is first referenced in the writings of Charles Lanman in the 1840s. Writing about the Cherokee Indians that lived in what is today Great Smoky Mountains National Park, he noted that they wrapped brightly colored feathers around a hook made of deer bone and secured the feathers to the hook with a strip of deer hide coated in some form of cement. It was also noted that the hackles were wrapped on the hook in a reverse fashion. The Cherokee would float the flies downstream and then impart a twitching or slight stripping motion as they retrieved the flies back upstream. This would cause the hackle to lay back along the fly as it was pulled and then the hackle would spring back into place as the fly was allowed to rest between twitches.

The Palmer was a staple of serious park anglers of the past like Mark Cathy, Fred Hall, and Eddie George. The heavy reverse hackle helps the fly to float high and dry. However, to this day there are still a few anglers that fish the Palmer as a wet fly,

The Yellow Palmer is believed to be the first fly that was ever produced or fished in the region. While today's versions are not tied on bone hooks with rawhide, they are nonetheless just as effective. The Palmer works as a caddis imitation as well as an all-around searching pattern.

The Orange Palmer is the most popular color variation and is highly effective in the fall.

and it still seems to work the same as it did nearly two hundred years ago.

Over the years, or centuries in the case of the Palmer, fly tiers have changed the pattern from its original form. What was at one time a bright-colored bird feather has been replaced with a dubbed body and combination of grizzly and brown hackle. You will find that the Palmer can be tied in just about every color. The most productive and common colors are yellow and orange. The other color I see around Great Smoky Mountains National Park occasionally is lime green, but it is not nearly as prevalent as the orange and yellow. The Orange Palmer tends to work best in the fall when the October Caddis are active or in the summer as an attractor for small native brook trout, while the Yellow Palmer tends to work best in the spring and early summer when the Yellow Sallies are most active.

Traditionally Palmers had no tail, and if anglers are going to fish them in the traditional manner of stripping the fly back upstream, I would suggest that you tie your Palmers with no tail. Most of the modern recipes call for a tail of either golden pheasant or a combination of brown and grizzly hackle fibers. I have also found that groundhog (aka woodchuck) makes a very nice tail

for the Palmer as well. If tiers want, they can swap the brown and grizzly hackle combination for either a cree hackle or a medium barred, dark ginger hackle.

There are several variations of the Palmer, but the most common is a fly called the Crackle Back. It too is tied with a reverse hackle and looks identical to the Palmer, with the exception that a small piece of peacock herl is added down the back of the fly prior to palmering the hackle forward. While this adds a lot of sex appeal to the fly in the bins of a shop, I have not found it to make a bit of difference to the trout, as they are looking at the bottom of the fly and rarely, if ever, get to see the peacock herl on the back.

When tying Palmers, tiers need to use caution to make sure that the hackle they are using is not more than one and a half times the gap of the hook. If the hackle is much more than one and a half times wider than the hook gap, it gets harder and harder to successfully hook fish on the fly. Tiers can also add a piece of extra-small wire counterwrapped over the hackle to reinforce the hackle and make the fly more durable.

Palmers have been used by anglers since fly fishing was introduced to the Smoky Mountains. I would chance to say that there is not a single old-school angler in the Smokies that doesn't still fish Palmers. PHOTO DAVID CANNON

Parachute Adams
- **Hook:** Daiichi 1170 or Mustad 94840 size 12-22
- **Thread:** Gray 6/0 Veevus
- **Tail:** Brown and grizzly hackle fibers
- **Body:** Gray poly dubbing
- **Post:** White calf tail
- **Hackle:** Grizzly and brown dry-fly hackle
- **Note:** For the Yellow Parachute Adams, use yellow poly or rabbit dubbing and a ginger hackle mixed with the grizzly. Other suitable hackle is a cree or medium barred ginger. To create a Female Adams Parachute, simply add a bright yellow egg sac to the back of the fly.

Parachute Adams

If there was one fly that I can guarantee is in the fly box of every trout angler in America, I would place my money on that fly being a Parachute Adams. So if you are reading this and don't have a Parachute Adams in your fly box, you need to either run to your local shop and pick some up or take up golf, whichever you prefer. Not only does everyone have a Parachute Adams in

their box, but I would be willing to bet that the vast majority of them are a size 14 to 18.

The Parachute Adams successfully represents nearly 80 percent of all mayfly duns. Over the years, I have caught trout, and plenty of them, on a Parachute Adams in every location that I have fished around the world with the one exception of Alaska. I am sure that at the right time it would

The Parachute Adams is the one fly that every trout angler in the country has in their vest and rightfully so, as it replicates the vast majority of mayfly duns. Over the years, the fish have gotten very accustomed to the size 14 and 16 Parachute Adams, and anglers may find more success using larger or smaller flies.

produce trout in Alaska, but I have always been there during the salmon spawning rush and the trout are gorging on salmon eggs. The trout in Great Smoky Mountains National Park are no exception, and they will take a Parachute Adams even when there is not a mayfly hatch taking place.

While writing this book, I called my good friends Captain Gary Taylor, Byron Begley, and J. E. B. Hall, all of whom have spent years fishing the streams of the Smokies. I asked them to name their top five flies for the park, and they all named the exact same five flies without having talked to each other. At the top of the list for all of them was the Parachute Adams.

I would venture to say that I have fished a Parachute Adams on every stream in the Smokies and the surrounding area that I have ever fished on. Most anglers, if you look in their box, will have Parachute Adamses in sizes 14 to 18. There is a time and place for those sizes, but over the last several years with so many people on the stream, I have found myself fishing different sizes. I fish a lot of size 10, 12, 18, and 20. The fish see so many size 14 and 16 Parachute Adamses these days that you can watch a fish float up under your fly and drift downstream with it while examining it. I have found that the trout don't see the large and smaller sizes as often and are not nearly as picky about a size 12 Parachute Adams as they are a size 14.

With the more-turbulent waters of the Great Smoky Mountains region, I highly suggest that anglers choose Parachute Adamses tied with a true calf tail post. Poly yarn and other synthetics make a good-looking fly but do not float as well as calf tail.

I was taught to tie parachutes by my uncle, Dwight Howell. He taught me a couple of tricks that make tying a parachute a little easier. First, we tie the parachute into the fly right after tying on the tail. This way you can use the calf tail under the body of the fly, which will help with flotation as well as make it easy to taper a body. Secondly, as soon as you have the parachute/post tied in, apply a drop of thin fly-tying head cement to the base of the parachute. By the time you build the body the glue will be dry and the base of the parachute will be stiff, and you can easily wrap the hackle around it without having the parachute flopping all over the place and the hackle sliding off the parachute. Finally, when you start hackling the parachute, start your first wrap as high as you will ever go on the parachute and then wrap each successive wrap under the previous wrap.

As for the various versions of the Parachute Adams, over the years I have tied and successfully fished a Parachute Female Adams and Yellow Parachute Adams is the park. The Parachute Female Adams is a great choice in March and April for anglers fishing an early spring spinner fall. The Yellow Parachute Adams will work better in May, June, and July when the Yellow Drakes, Sulphurs, and Little Yellow Stoneflies are abundant.

The Yellow Parachute Adams is most effective during the yellow mayfly and sulphur hatches.

While a Parachute Adams will catch fish on every stream in the park, anglers still have to have a stealthy approach and spot-on presentation in the clear waters of the Smokies to be highly successful.

Red Fox Squirrel Nymph (Beadhead)

- **Hook:** #8-18 Daiichi 1710 or Mustad 9671
- **Bead:** Gold, sized to hook
- **Thread:** Rusty brown 6/0 Veevus
- **Abdomen:** SLF Whitlock's Red Fox Squirrel Abdomen Dubbing
- **Thorax:** SLF Whitlock's Red Fox Squirrel Thorax Dubbing
- **Rib:** Gold oval tinsel
- **Tail:** Red fox squirrel back fur
- **Collar:** Speckled partridge
- **Note:** For a non-bead-head version, simply weight the hook shank with the desired size of lead. Tiers may also prefer to use pearl tinsel as a substitute for the gold oval tinsel.

Red Fox Squirrel Nymph

The Red Fox Squirrel Nymph was designed by Dave Whitlock. Dave's fly was created by accident, or so he claims, but it is one of the few flies that cross all barriers. Depending on how it is tied, it can replicate caddis or mayfly larvae as well as small crustaceans.

My introduction to the Red Fox Squirrel Nymph (RFSN) was in the mid-1980s by my uncle Dwight Howell. He had fished with Dave and came home raving about the success of the nymph. He and I went fishing on the North Fork of the Toe River, and he rigged me up with a RFSN. I caught several fish on the fly as we went up the river, but it really did not seem to shine all that bright to me. Nearly ten years went by, and I did not think a whole lot about the fly. It was right after my father's passing in 1998 on a trip with my good friend John Brinkley that I rediscovered it.

John and I went fishing on the Oconaluftee at the edge of the park. After going through our normal fly selection, we were struggling

The Beadhead Red Fox Squirrel Nymph (above fly tied by Montana Fly Company) can be effectively fished as both a caddis pupa or a mayfly nymph. Anytime you find a nymph that effectively represents multiple food sources, such as this one, you will find a fly that will work year-round.

Beadhead Rubber Leg Red Fox Squirrel Nymph

to catch a few fish. I got to noticing spent Yellow Mayflies from the day before in the spiderwebs hanging over the stream. I told John we needed something that looked like a Hendrickson or Yellow Drake Nymph. Digging through my box, I found a Beadhead Red Fox Squirrel Nymph; we tied it on and immediately started catching fish.

That day was the start of my belief in the RFSN. As a guide, I am always looking for flies that are impressionistic and lifelike in the water. I am also looking for flies that even if a client does not have the best presentation, the trout are still willing to strike. The RFSN has several key factors that meet all of the above criteria. The soft hackle gives it life (movement) in the water without being obnoxious. The squirrel hair is coarse and spiky, which traps air bubbles, causing the fly to look like a molting or lively insect larva. The SLF blend then adds just enough flash and sparkle to the fly to interest every trout in the river, regardless of how lethargic they may be. As a guide, the RFSN has become one of my go-to flies and is often the fly I start and end the trip with.

There are several variations to the Red Fox Squirrel Nymph, including a caddis version tied on a scud hook, the bead-head version, a rubber leg version, and one that Dave calls The Crustacean; regardless of the version, I have found them all to be highly effective. In the last few years I have even been tying my RFSNs on a jig hook with a tungsten bead. I have seen the fly tied with either small or extra-small gold oval tinsel or pearl Flashabou for the rib. I fish and tie both versions, though I do feel that performance-wise, the pearl Flashabou edges out the gold tinsel slightly.

When tying any version of the Red Fox Squirrel Nymph, sourcing the proper material is key to success. The tail of the fly is constructed from hair from the back of a red fox squirrel hide. Squirrels that have been harvested during the late fall and winter make not only the best tailing material but also the best dubbing due to their thick winter coats. When tying in the soft-hackle collar, less is more. I take the hackle I am going to use and strip the barbs off the underside and then hackle the fly. This tends to allow the hackle to breathe and flow better while in the water.

Red Fox Squirrel Nymphs work well in the spring for both caddis and mayfly nymphs. High-sticking them around and behind large boulders will produce lots of Smoky Mountain rainbows. PHOTO DAVID CANNON

Sheepfly

Sheepfly

- **Hook:** #6-14 Daiichi 2220
- **Thread:** Black or brown 6/0 Veevus
- **Collar:** Brown hackle (typically strung rooster neck feathers)
- **Body:** Blend of dark gray rabbit and muskrat back with guard hairs left in
- **Underbody:** Lead wire (.035)
- **Tail:** Hackle fibers from a brown rooster feather
- **Wings:** Grizzly hackle tips from a light-cast domestic Dominique chicken

Originated by the late Newland Saunders of Lenoir, North Carolina, the Sheepfly was a favored fly of the late George "Cap" Wiese, who was the headmaster at the Penland School. Cap was responsible for introducing the Sheepfly to my father, Don R. Howell, and uncle Dwight Howell on the banks of the Linville River in Ashe County, North Carolina. From that moment on, the fly was a favorite of my father's, who is responsible for introducing the fly to the rest of the world. Toward the end of his life when asked what his favorite trout fly was, he would reply, "If I could only have one fly

to trout fish with the rest of my life, it would be the Sheepfly."

Right before his passing, I had the opportunity to sit down with Newland and talk at length as fishermen do about fly designs, fishing trips, and, of course, the one that got away. I asked him what his inspiration for the fly had been and how it got its name. Newland stated that when he returned home from World War II, he spent many days fishing Helton and Wilson Creeks. Since flies and tying materials were hard to come by those days, especially in rural southern Appalachia, he used the materials that he had available,

While the Sheepfly looks homely and misplaced and does not really represent any food source, it is known to produce very large trout and lots of them. My father often said if he had to choose one fly to fish with the rest of his life, the Sheepfly would be it.

which were mainly furs and hairs from trapping and hunting or feathers from the chickens in the yard. Hence a simple gray dubbed body of muskrat and rabbit fur, a collar of brown hackle from a Rhode Island Red, and grizzly wings made from feathers plucked from the Dominique chicken. This simple combination would lead to one of the most famous of all southern Appalachian trout flies. When I asked Newland how he came up with the name, he simply stated, "It looked like the flies buzzing around my sheep's ass."

While the Sheepfly produces vast numbers of trout, for some reason it produces more large trout than any other fly I know of. I have personally caught hundreds of trout over 20 inches on the humble Sheepfly. My father, uncle, and fellow guides have also caught countless large fish on the Sheepfly, including a 31-inch, 10-pound behemoth that my father caught out of the Oconaluftee River in Great Smoky Mountains National Park in 1991. For years I tried to figure out what the Sheepfly imitates, and while it really does not look like much of anything, I have come to believe that most fish take it for large crane fly larvae.

While the Sheepfly was originally tied on a 1X-long nymph hook, my father and Cap Wiese typically tied their versions on a 4X- or 6X-long nymph hook. I typically tie the Sheepfly in sizes 4 to 12, with a size 8 4X-long streamer hook my preferred size. Tiers should weight the shank of the hook with lead wire; while I carry several different weights with me, my favored weight for the Smokies is sixteen turns of .030 or .035 lead wire on the size 8 4X-long hook.

The original dubbing is a mix of muskrat back and gray rabbit, but over the years my father and I have experimented with every color and dubbing blend I could think of. We have also added flash to the dubbing and have done everything we could think of to sexy the fly up and make it catch more fish. To this day, we have not found a better fish producer than the original gray, drab Sheepfly. It is crucial when tying the Sheepfly that the body ends up shaped like a football, pointed on both ends and fat in the middle. This allows the wings and collar to lie back over the body of the fly. The collar and wings should lie back about three-fourths of the hook shank.

The Sheepfly is effective 365 days a year. It was the favored fly of both my father and Cap Wiese, both of them often refered to it as the only fly you needed for trout in the Smoky Mountains.
PHOTO J. E. B. HALL

Slump Buster

Slump Buster (Olive)

- **Hook:** #6-10 Daiichi 1720 or Mustad 9672
- **Cone:** Gold, sized to hook
- **Thread:** Black Veevus PB 140 denier
- **Body:** Sparkle Braid olive
- **Rib:** Wire gold (brassie)
- **Wing:** Olive pine squirrel strip
- **Collar:** Olive pine squirrel strip, wrapped

A fly that lives up to its reputation, John Barr's Slump Buster was originally distributed by Umpqua Feather Merchants in the early 2000s. The fly made use of two materials that were new at the time, a heavy tungsten conehead and a pine squirrel Zonker, and because of the Slump Buster's success, these materials have become synonymous with fly fishing.

The funny thing about the fly is that John Barr and I had both submitted similar patterns to my friend Bruce Olson at Umpqua. I used lead dumbbell eyes instead of the tungsten cone and did not have a flashy-looking body—my pattern was more of a Double Bunny style of fly. Bruce called and told me they were going with John's pattern over mine, and once I saw John's fly, I knew I would have made the same decision. Bruce had shared a few of the samples with me once they arrived back from the Umpqua factory, and I started fishing the pattern almost immediately.

Streamer fishing in the smaller streams of the Appalachian Mountains is very difficult but can be productive if you can find the right fly. Since it is all but impossible to cast a sinking or sink-tip line on the smaller

The Olive Slump Buster is one of the best streamers that anglers can have in their box when the fish get picky. So often people think that streamers need to be 5 or 6 inches or bigger, when in reality the majority of minnows and daces that the trout are feeding on are 2 inches or less.

streams, you have to rely solely on the ability of the fly to sink quickly. This can be a challenge, as the larger the profile of the fly, the more it rides up in the water column.

On one of the first trips I used the Slump Buster, I was guiding two anglers from South Carolina, Jim and Bob. Both were experienced and I had guided them many times prior and knew they were capable of putting the fly where it needed to go. We rounded the bend on one of the streams in the park, and lying in the tail of the pool was a brown trout that weighed every bit of 12 pounds. We slowly worked into position for a cast. I had them go into the woods and rock-paper-scissors to see who was going to be the person that got to cast to the fish. Jim won the contest, and I rigged his rod with an Olive Slump Buster. He made the cast and on the second strip the trout charged the fly and inhaled it all in one motion. As I yelled "Set!" at the top of my lungs, Jim stood motionless, no fish on his line, and said, "That was the coolest thing I have ever seen." Bob and I in unison said, "It would have been a lot cooler if you had set the hook."

The trout went right back to where he had been lying, just like nothing had happened. So I rigged Bob with a tan-colored Slump Buster and he made a cast, and again on the second strip of the fly it was like the trout was headed for Mars—he rushed the fly and inhaled it. This time Bob stood motionless, having never set the hook. We all watched as the large trout slowly sank into the depths of the pool. I spent the remainder of the season fishing for that brown but never saw him again. I often figure he died of old age and returns to haunt the dreams of many anglers, including Jim and Bob. They still fish with me today, and I remind them at the beginning of every trip how to set the hook.

Slump Busters are relatively easy to tie. One thing I would caution against is making the fly too heavy; tiers should consider how much weight is added to the fly once the Zonker is wet. If you wrap lead wire on the hook shank and use the tungsten cone, it can be very difficult to cast on 4- and 5-weight rods. You can tie Slump Busters with the new Micro Pulsator Strips from Hareline Dubbin, but I do feel that pine squirrel makes the best fly.

Streamers like the Slump Buster are most effective when they are cast across the current and retrieved across and up against the current. Large pools offer better streamer fishing than the broken swift water in the Smokies.
PHOTO DAVID CANNON

Smoky Mountain Candy
- **Hook:** Mustad 94840 size 10-16
- **Thread:** Uni-Thread 6/0 Rusty Brown
- **Body:** Dirty yellow dubbing
- **Tail:** White-tailed deer
- **Wing:** Calftail white
- **Hackle:** Brown and grizzly dry fly hackle

Smoky Mountain Candy

The Smoky Mountain Candy was originated by friend and fellow fly tier Walter Babb. He used to tie them commercially for Little River Outfitters, until his rod-building business got to be too big and he simply could not spare the time to tie them for LRO any longer. Walter, like myself, has spent the majority of his life walking and fishing the streams in and around Great Smoky Mountains National Park. He understands everything that goes into making a highly productive fly for the Smokies.

Over the years, most of the great Smoky Mountain patterns have had a few things in common. Most of them have featured a mixed grizzly and brown hackle, and a lot of them have a yellow (yallar) body. And all of them make use of large calf tail wings, which aid with flotation and make them easy to spot on the water. Walter's Smoky Mountain Candy incorporates all those properties.

The first time I saw the fly was when my good friend Byron Begley of Little River Outfitters invited me over for a tying

Walter Babb has logged more time on the streams of the Smokies than most people have spent at work. His vast knowledge of the fisheries and interactions with the trout led him to develop one of the most prominent flies of the region, the Smoky Mountain Candy.

demonstration. During a break I was roaming around the store and looking at flies and saw the Smoky Mountain Candy in one of the fly bins. When I asked Byron about the fly, he said it was something that Walter had come up with and it had really been catching fish. I picked up a couple of them, mainly as a pattern, and put the flies in the truck.

A few days later I was guiding my good friend and client Reverend Mark Wilson on the North Fork of the Mills River just outside of Asheville, North Carolina. As we were preparing to walk into the stream, I realized that I had left my box of dry flies at home on my tying bench, where I had been working the day before. I scrounged around the truck and found a couple of small hoppers and the box with the two Smoky Mountain Candies in it. As a guide, you never want to admit you have forgotten or misplaced a crucial part of your gear—it doesn't really inspire confidence in your clients. So with the utmost confidence in Walter's fly, I told Mark that this was a new pattern and had really been catching fish, as if that had been my plan all along.

Midsize streams like the North Mills are an excellent choice for dry-fly fishing. PHOTO DR. PATRICK WILLIAMS

As we started up the stream, it did not take long until Reverend Wilson was hooked up. As the day progressed, he caught nearly thirty fish, all on the Smoky Mountain Candy. I am not sure if it was divine intervention or my overpowering confidence in the fly simply because it was the only dry fly I had at the moment. It was years later after Mark and I had become really close that I confessed to him that I had forgotten one of my fly boxes that day and that we had started and continued fishing those flies because it was all I had for dry flies.

Since then, I have fished the Smoky Mountain Candy with a lot of confidence and it has never failed to produce on all the streams throughout the region. I have noticed that the fly tends to produce better during times of higher water and just after thunderstorms when the water has a slight tea color to it, which is almost a daily event in the Smoky Mountains during the summer months.

The tail of the fly aids in flotation, so I prefer to use hair from the back of a whitetail deer. This hair is darker and stiffer in nature and helps the fly float. I have used, and have seen Walter use, woodchuck (groundhog) for a tail and it works fine if the deer hair is not available. You also will have to blend your dubbing to be a dirty yellow color. While the recipe calls for synthetic dubbing, I prefer to use rabbit for its buggy appearance and the fact that I can easily manipulate the color. I start with pure rabbit dubbing in bright yellow and small amounts of tan and brown until I get a dirty yellow-brown color of dubbing.

Smoky Mountain Forked Tail
- **Hook:** Daiichi 1170 or Mustad 94840 size 10-16
- **Thread:** Dun gray 6/0 UNI-Thread
- **Tail:** Dun goose biots
- **Body:** Sulphur orange or slate gray dubbing
- **Wings:** Gray hackle tips or gray matched duck quill wings
- **Hackle:** Medium dyed dun

Smoky Mountain Forked Tail

If there is one fly from the Great Smoky Mountains that is wrapped in mystery and confusion, it would have to be the Smoky Mountain Forked Tail. The Forked Tail seems to exist as both a dry fly and a wet fly, depending on whom you talk with. Furthermore, no one seems to know anything about its origin. The other obstacle is that depending on the tier and the location in the park, it is tied in a multitude of colors, all claiming to be the correct or only color you need. Even more disputed is the wing

and tail configuration. So for the purpose of this book, I have gone with the pattern that I was taught from an early age.

Roger Lowe referenced the pattern with an orange body, while Don Kirk referenced it with an orange or tan body. For my entire life, most of the Forked Tails I have seen from the old-timers featured a grayish-brown body. I think, but cannot confirm, that the fly is possibly an offshoot of the fly called the Queen of the Water, which also was available in both a dry-fly and wet-fly

The Smoky Mountain Forked Tail is a fly of myth and legend—no one is sure of its origin or creator. It is also a fly known by many local old-timers to be a consistent producer. If you are looking to fish a classic fly pattern that is shrouded in myth and lore but still produces fish, give the Smoky Mountain Forked Tail a try.

version with an orange body and a similar wing style. The Queen of the Water was a popular pattern in the region and is featured in Ray Bergman's book *Trout Flies*.

Regardless of its origins, every old-timer I have ever talked to spoke of the pattern as if it had the same magical powers as Excalibur (King Arthur's sword) that caused the trout to just roll over and float to the top for the angler to pick up. My great-uncle swore that it was the only fly you needed and was the only one that would catch fish. Over my many years of commercial fly tying, I will say I have tied hundreds of dozens of Smoky Mountain Forked Tails in both the orange- and gray-colored bodies. But until this book came along, I had never fished the fly. I knew it should be featured in the book because of its mysterious history and the siren-song properties I had always heard of, but did not feel comfortable putting the fly in the book without having fished it. So I tied some up and put a few in my box and a few in the hands of some trusted anglers that I know frequent the Smokies.

My time on the water with the Smoky Mountain Forked Tail, while short, proved

Orange Smoky Mountain Forked Tail

to be fruitful. I started with the fly on some high-elevation brook trout streams and found that the brookies much preferred the orange body over the gray body. Moving to lower-elevation streams, I found that the rainbow trout preferred the gray-bodied Forked Tail over the orange. I did manage to catch a couple of brown trout, but they were not nearly as impressed by the fly as the rainbows and brookies. When I talked with a friend I had given some Forked Tails to, he reported that he found the rainbow trout ate the orange- and gray-bodied flies with equal enthusiasm. I do feel that the orange body will be productive on brown trout in the fall during the October Caddis hatch.

When it comes to tying the Smoky Mountain Forked Tail, as discussed earlier, the body can be either orange, gray, or tan, but orange and gray are the most prominent. I prefer to use regular rabbit dubbing without guard hairs for the body dubbing. For the tail I use gray goose biots, splayed apart. The wings are another area of contention: I prefer to use medium dun hackle tips, but I have seen plenty tied with matched duck quill wings. I have found the duck quill to be far more fragile, however, not to mention a royal pain to tie in. I have also seen the fly tied with wood duck as well as mallard flank wings.

I found that the orange Forked Tail worked best in the fall and on the high-elevation streams, while the gray body worked best in the spring and in lower elevations. PHOTO DR. PATRICK WILLIAMS

**Soft Hackle
Pheasant Tail**

- **Hook:** #12-20
  Daiichi 1550 or
  Mustad 3906
- **Thread:** Brown
  70-denier Ultra
  Thread
- **Body:** Pheasant tail
- **Thorax:** Peacock
  Ice Dub
- **Hackle:** Hungarian
  partridge
- **Note:** Tiers can
  substitute starling
  or soft-hackle
  hen's back for
  the collar hackle
  if Hungarian
  partridge is not
  available.

Soft Hackle Pheasant Tail

Any fly pattern that has survived over two hundred years and has an entire book written about it is probably a fly that you should have in your fly box regardless of where you live or fish. In his book *Two Centuries of Soft Hackled Flies*, Sylvester Nemes traced the history of the soft hackle all the way back to 1794. As a guide, I have always carried soft hackles in my fly box. They are almost impossible to fish incorrectly—trout will even eat them when you have a bad presentation.

I became particularly fond of the Soft Hackle Pheasant Tail during my days of competitive fishing. In 2006, at the Fly Fishing Masters Invitational event in Pennsylvania, my partner Rick Hartman and I were given a box of six flies. We could not use any of our personal flies during the event until we had caught at least one fish on one of the six flies we had been given by the tournament director. So we picked the big Woolly Bugger–looking streamer out, and sure enough, on the third cast it hung and broke off. A few casts later, the other

Soft hackles have been in existence for over two hundred years. They can be fished on the swing as an emerging mayfly or caddis presentation, or dead drifted deep in the water column. Every serious guide I know relies heavily on Soft Hackle Pheasant Tails at different times throughout the year.

streamer was hung and broken off on the bottom of the Little Juniata River.

Almost an hour into the two-and-a-half-hour competition, we were still struggling to catch a fish on the flies they had given us. So I looked at Rick, opened the box, and tied on the Soft Hackle Pheasant Tail. I told Rick that I was going to fish the riffle and was going to catch a rainbow on the soft hackle so we could fish our own flies. Rick argued that the fish would be small and I agreed, but I thought we could still score three more fish and use any flies we had in our box to catch them. So I ran to the riffle, made a long cast, and about halfway through the drift hooked a big fish, which came off. On the second cast I ended up landing a decent-sized rainbow.

Finally we could fish our own flies, and we ended up winning the morning session. We went on to win the Fly Fishing Masters National Championship that year, all because of my decision to fish that small Soft Hackle Pheasant Tail.

The beauty of a soft hackle is that it is almost impossible to fish incorrectly. You can swing it, dead drift it, strip it, crawl it—it really does not matter how you present it, the fish will still eat it. Soft hackles excel

The yellow version of the soft hackle is great for fishing the PMD and yellow mayfly hatches.

Swinging soft hackles where a riffle first dumps into a pool is effective anytime the caddis are active. Soft hackles can also be fished just under the film as an emerger. PHOTO DAVID CANNON

during caddis hatches, especially if anglers fish them in the traditional method by swinging them down and across the current. I also use them a lot when fish are nymphing just below the surface; very seldom will you have a trout refuse a properly presented soft hackle in this situation. Since the addition of beads to the tier's arsenal, anglers can get soft hackles tied with glass, brass, or tungsten beads. This has allowed anglers to experiment with new presentations, like Euro nymphing with soft-hackle-style flies.

The key to tying a good soft hackle is the quality and quantity of the hackle used to tie the collar. Of all the materials I have seen used, Hungarian partridge and starling make the best soft hackles. With other materials like speckled hen's back, tiers will need to strip one side of the material off of the shank of the feather prior to wrapping it; otherwise, the hackle will be very thick and webby and will cling to itself instead of breathing and swimming in the current. In the last few years I have started using Veevus Body Quill instead of pheasant tail It seems to give the fly a little more sparkle and life without overpowering the fly with too much flash.

Sparkle Minnow

Sparkle Minnow Sculpin
- **Hook:** #4-8 Daiichi 2220 or Mustad 79580
- **Thread:** White Veevus PB 140 denier
- **Head:** Black cone, sized to match hook
- **Tail:** White, cream, and olive marabou, layered together
- **Body:** Gold Wing N' Flash, twisted into a brush
- **Belly:** Pearl Wing N' Flash, twisted into a brush and pulled tight across bottom of fly
- **Note:** Use a black Sharpie or Pantone marker to color the back of the fly. For the single-color Sparkle Minnow, just make a dubbing brush with the desired color of Wing N' Flash.

Sometimes it is curiosity that kills the cat, or in this instance the trout. Many years ago noted angler Chuck Kraft developed a fly called the Kreelex Minnow for use on West Virginia's New River for smallmouth bass. The Kreelex Minnow was simply gold Kreelex flash over top of silver Kreelex flash with a set of dumbbell eyes. It was highly effective for bass. Over the years, I experimented with the fly and caught other species on it. Then on a Montana trip in the early 2000s, I was introduced to the Coffey's Sparkle Minnow. The Sparkle Minnow had a gold and pearl flash body similar to the Kreelex, but with an added marabou tail that gave it significantly more life in the water. Over the course of the trip, I caught a lot of fish on the fly on the Jefferson and Madison Rivers.

When I returned home in early October, I came back to high, off-color rivers—that

The Sparkle Minnow Sculpin (above fly tied by Montana Fly Company) is just as deadly on the smallmouth bass found in the Smokies as on the trout. It is especially effective on bright, sunny days when the trout can key in on the flash from a long distance away.

year it seemed to rain a lot in Western North Carolina. October is the start of the state's delayed harvest season, and with the water higher than normal, I spent most of that fall streamer fishing with clients on the Tuckasegee River. After a few days of fishing, the trout started to get a little picky. While rummaging through my streamer box, I found a couple of the Sparkle Minnows that I had been using in Montana. The trout seemed to run out of their way to attack the Sparkle Minnow.

The problem was, the fly was being tied out west and was not available on the East Coast at that point in time. So I took my last Sparkle Minnow and cut it apart so that I could figure out how to tie some up. After a few hours at the vise, I was resupplied with Sparkle Minnows. I guided all that fall with Sparkle Minnows and not only found them to be highly effective on stocked trout, but they also worked very well on the wild trout of Western North Carolina and East Tennessee. As we rolled into late spring and I started guiding for smallmouth, I gave the Sparkle Minnow a try and found it to be equally effective on smallmouth in and around the Smokies. The following year the fly had become so popular that Montana Fly Company picked it

up and started producing it, and it found its way into fly shops across the country.

When fishing for trout around Great Smoky Mountains National Park, I prefer to fish the original sculpin color with a conehead in a size 6. In lower, clear water conditions, I switch to a size 8 bead-head version in white or light olive. For bass I prefer either a size 4 in the original pattern or a jigged version tied with a Fish-Skull head on a size 1/0 jig hook. I use the jig version mainly in the early fall when the baitfish are at their largest and I am trying to replicate a 4- or 5-inch shad or herring.

While the original pattern was called the Sculpin Sparkle Minnow and had a tricolor marabou tail, a gold-over-pearl body with a black back, and a conehead, today there are countless variations of the pattern. The most common are the white, light olive, brown, black, and pink color variations and a bead head. There are also versions tied on jig hooks and even articulated versions.

When tying the Sparkle Minnow, tiers will find that dubbing brushes either produced by Montana Fly Company or made yourself make tying the fly much easier. Once the tail is in place, both the gold and pearl dubbing brushes are tied on. The gold brush is wound forward, creating the gold body. The pearl brush is then pulled forward on the bottom of the fly as the belly. The black back is created by taking a black Sharpie to the top of the gold dubbing brush.

White Sparkle Minnow (tied by Montana Fly Company)

Zach Hart employs the fast-sinking Sparkle Minnow in large plunge pools to entice Smoky Mountain trout.

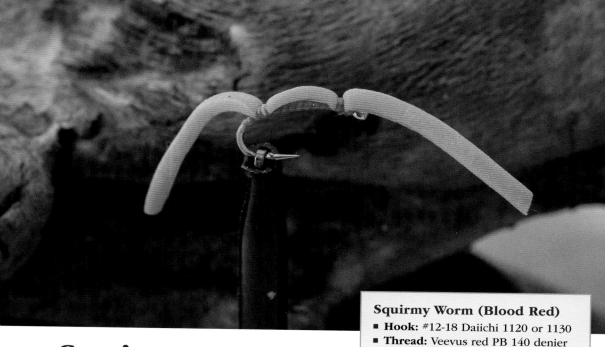

Squirmy Worm

Squirmy Worm (Blood Red)
- **Hook:** #12-18 Daiichi 1120 or 1130
- **Thread:** Veevus red PB 140 denier
- **Body:** Bright-red Caster's Squirmito

After its conception in the late 1960s, it did not take long for the San Juan Worm to find a home in every fly box in the world. Every guide knew its powers, as did every competitive angler. The Squirmy Worm has its beginnings in the world of competitive trout fishing, as every competitive angler is always trying to find an edge over other anglers.

My introduction to any type of plastic-made San Juan Worm came at the Harman's North Fork Invitational Tournament in West Virginia. My teammate and good friend Walker Parrott and I were roaming around a little shop in Cabins and noticed a bright pink dog toy with long tentacles lying in a sale bin. We grabbed the toy, purchased it, and stuffed it into a pocket so no one else could see it. Back in the safety of our cabin, we quickly cut a tentacle off of the toy, put a bright-red tungsten bead on a hook, and tied the plastic tentacle directly behind the bead to make it a jig-style fly.

After a quick conference with the tournament director, it was deemed legal as a fly and off we went. During the second fishing session, we broke pinky out of the bag and scored our four fish in almost record time. By the time we arrived back at the staging area, the news of our creation had already reached the rest of the crowd. In fairness, we decided to make part of the toy available to the rest of the competitors. Most balked

The Squirmy Worm (Blood Red variation shown here) is a modern adaptation of the San Juan Worm, which is a known fish producer. The Squirmy Worm offers more movement than the San Juan as well as more-vivid color options. Because of its flexible body and movement, the Squirmy can be tied on jig-style hooks and made to stand up off the bottom.

and scoffed at the idea, but a few took us up on the offer.

About the same time, Dave Caster in Hickory, North Carolina, was experimenting with silicone worms as well. Dave managed to find a reliable source for the material, as opposed to us cutting up dog toys. In less than two years, the Squirmy Worm went from conception to being in every fly shop and every fly box in the nation.

With all of the colors available, I have found that you can fish a Squirmy Worm in the streams in and around Great Smoky Mountains National Park literally any day of the year in almost any water condition. The bright green colors make for excellent inchworm imitations during the spring and summer months. In low, clear water situations, the clear worms can be used to fool the park's wary fish. In times of high water, I have fished black Squirmy Worms, but my favorite colors are the bright pink and the blood red, as they look more realistic in the water.

Over the years, several versions of the Squirmy have been developed. The most common is tied just like a San Juan Worm, while the second most common version is tied on a jig-style hook with a bead head

The beginnings of the Squirmy revolution from dog toy to fishing lure.

and the worm is left long in the back and tends to stand up on the bottom.

While it is a simple pattern, there is a learning curve to tying Squirmy Worms. Tiers should use a 140-denier thread that lies flat on the hook; this will help prevent tiers from cutting the worms in half when tying them to the hook. Tiers should never glue the thread on Squirmy Worms, as this interaction of glue and silicone will cause the worm to dissolve and will actually melt the worm in half. I go as far as to never store my worms with other flies that have been glued in order to prevent this interaction. In place of the glued thread, I use a triple whip finish to secure my thread. The final hurdle will be getting the worm on the hook itself—be sure to build a thread base on the hook to prevent the worm from rolling around the hook.

If tiers want to add weight to the fly, there are a couple of options. Those who want to use wire can wrap the shank of the hook with the wire and then use thread to cover the wire before they secure the worm to the hook. For those who prefer to tie with beads, there are a couple ways to add the bead to the fly. The most common method is to place the bead on the hook and use thread fore and aft to secure the bead to the hook, then drape the worm over the bead and secure it to the hook on each side of the bead. The other method is to take a bobbin threader and push it through the hole in the bead, then use the threader to pull the worm through the bead. Then place the hook through the bead as normal, with the worm through the bead as well. Once the hook and worm are through the bead, use your tying thread to secure the worm and bead to the hook shank on each side of the bead.

Stickbait
- **Hook:** #8-14 Mustad 37160 or Daiichi 1260
- **Thread:** Black 140-denier Ultra Thread
- **Underbody:** Lead wire overwrapped with cream-colored yarn to build desired body thickness
- **Body:** Cream latex
- **Head:** Black rabbit dubbing with guard hairs

Stickbait

Growing up in the Great Smoky Mountains National Park region, there were three baits that every trout fisherman talked about: stickbait, wasp larva, and grampus. To the uninitiated, a stickbait is a caddis larva that builds its nest in sticks, the wasp larvae was what they gathered from a wasp nest that they had somehow exterminated, and a grampus is the larva of the dobsonfly (aka hellgrammite). My grandfather showed me at an early age how to collect grampus and stickbait from the river and use them as bait. It does not take long for an angler using stickbait to collect a limit of trout.

Stickbait is so sought after by trout that I have seen them eat the entire stick nest in times of high water. So it was inevitable that a fly would be created to replicate this highly productive food source. The Stickbait nymph was a favorite of the late Benny Joe Craig from Waynesville, North Carolina, as well as countless other older fly fishermen around the Smokies.

In Great Smoky Mountains National Park there are several forms of caddis larvae, but

The original Stickbait pattern tied on a Mustad 37160 hook was a favorite nymph of most of the old-school nymph fishermen around the park. The fly originated from the caddis pupae that anglers would strip out of the stick-built nest and use as bait before fly fishing became popular.

what is referred to as stickbait is the larvae of the October Caddis; they are large in nature, anywhere from a size 14 all the way up to a size 8. This is a fly that is so simple yet so specific that it has escaped the tinkerings of fly tiers.

I have fished the Stickbait in just about every scenario that you can imagine, but have found that it fishes best during times of high off-color water and in riffles. I feel this is due to the fact that the higher water flows are stirring things around on the bottom, and this is when the majority of the nest and caddis larvae get dislodged and become available to the trout. During the summer months, just about every afternoon you can count on a thunderstorm in the Great Smoky Mountains region. In lower-water years especially, I have seen the trout lie and wait for a thunderstorm to bring the water level up, and they will then feed heavily for a few hours. Then once the water recedes, they will stop feeding until the thunderstorm the next afternoon. During these times of higher water, there are three flies that seem to produce fish with reckless abandon—a Stickbait, a stonefly, and a

Riffles like the famed Caddis Riffle on the Watauga River are the best places for anglers to start fishing this old mountain classic, especially during times of higher water flows.

hellgrammite—because the naturals are all being swept downstream by the increased current. I have also found that the Stickbait nymph produces fish better on the midsize to large streams as opposed to the smaller, higher-elevation streams. Over the years, I have found this fly to be especially effective on the Oconaluftee, Cataloochee, Hazel Creek, and Deep Creek drainages.

Tying the Stickbait is super easy—it is simply a latex strip wrapped around a hook with a dubbed black head at the front. I have seen the fly tied on several different hooks but have found that hooks with a slight curve like the Daiichi model 1260 or 1770 work best. The old-timer anglers only wanted it tied on a Mustad 37160. I tend to weight the fly heavily because the natural larvae are not free swimmers and you are often fishing higher, more turbid water. I prefer the versions without a bead head, but when I do tie and fish a bead-head version, I tend to use a black tungsten bead and let it make up the majority of the nymph's head.

Stickbait tied on a modern Daiichi curved-style hook.

Yellow Rubber Leg Stimulator

- **Hook:** #10-18 Daiichi 1270
- **Thread:** Orange 70-denier Ultra Thread
- **Tail:** Yearling elk
- **Abdomen:** Yellow Antron dubbing
- **Abdomen hackle:** Brown dry-fly hackle
- **Wing:** Yearling elk
- **Thorax:** Fire orange Antron dubbing
- **Thorax hackle:** Grizzly dry-fly hackle
- **Rib:** Copper wire (fine)
- **Legs:** White Flexi Floss (medium)

Stimulator

The history of the Stimulator is a little shaky. Many believe that Randall Kaufmann, the renowned fly tier and shop owner, invented it. However, the fly is also said to have originated on the Musconetcong River in New Jersey by tier Jim Slattery as a stonefly imitation and was named the Stimulator after a punk rock band. My guess is that Kaufmann refined the fly and had the distribution channel to send it to a level of national attention—much like my father is often credited with the invention of the Sheepfly, which was actually developed by Newland Saunders.

Regardless of who created the fly, I would chance to say that it can be found in the fly boxes of almost every fly angler in the world. The Stimulator serves a dual role in those boxes: It represents not only a stonefly or a little Sally in the park region but also a caddis in smaller sizes, and sometimes I think trout take it for a large terrestrial or land-born insect that just ended up in the river.

The Yellow Rubber Leg Stimulator (above fly tied by Montana Fly Company) is the most popular modern dry-fly pattern purchased by anglers headed to the Smokies. While most anglers choose it for use as a general searching/attractor pattern, it also is an excellent choice for the many Yellow Sallies encountered in the Smokies. It is also a great choice for rigging dry-dropper rigs.

With an elk hair tail and underbody, an elk hair wing, and a heavy hackle that runs across both the abdomen and thorax, it is almost unsinkable. This floatability made the Stimulator a favorite among Smoky Mountain anglers. It was one of the first dry flies used in the region that truly represented a Little Yellow Stonefly. Because of how well it floats, it continues to be a perennial favorite during late spring and early summer when the Yellow Sallies are most active. The Stimulator was also quickly recognized as one of the best flies on the market for dry-dropper fishing.

My good friend Woody Platt (yes, of the Steep Canyon Rangers) used to guide for me at Davidson River Outfitters before his musical career took off. Woody was, and still to this day is, an exceptional fly angler and very attentive to new trends and flies on the market. He was an excellent guide, and was an early adopter of the Stimulator in our region. Woody fished the Stimulator with clients so much that I am not sure he even had another dry fly in his box, and if he did, I am sure that it had a rusty hook because it never saw the light of day. Woody simply changed the color of the body and the size he was using with the season.

Stimulators can be tied in countless different color combinations, and I would recommend that park anglers carry at least three different colors with them on the stream. I use a yellow Stimulator in the spring and summer to imitate the Little Yellow Stoneflies (aka Yellow Sallies). In the summer months I especially like to use Stimulators with rubber legs added, as I feel this gives the fly a little extra draw. In the fall I use an orange- or ginger-bodied Stimulator to imitate the October Caddis that are common on area streams. In the winter months I use a jet-black Stimulator to imitate the black winter stoneflies found throughout the region from November through February.

When tying the Stimulator, the quality of the elk hair is the key to a great fly. I have found that yearling elk makes the best Stimulators. If yearling elk is not available, I like to use bull elk from bow harvest before they put on their heavy winter coat.

As for variations, the rubber leg Stimulator is prominently available as are countless body colors. I primarily carry the rubber leg version in my fly box and if the fish are fussy about the legs, I will simply pull them out of the fly.

The Black Stimulator is most effective November through February when the little winter stoneflies are most active.

The Royal Stimulator makes a great searching pattern for the summer months.

Strawberry Blonde

Strawberry Blonde
- **Hook:** #4-12 Daiichi 2220 or Mustad 79580
- **Bead:** Red metallic tungsten, sized to hook
- **Thread:** Light Cahill 6/0 Veevus
- **Tail:** Cream, brown, and black strung marabou, rolled together
- **Hackle:** Barred ginger
- **Body:** Brown and yellow variegated chenille (medium)

The Strawberry Blonde was developed on the banks of the Watauga River in East Tennessee. While guiding on the Watauga, I would often see trout chasing bait, especially during times of generation of high water. Over several years, I tried several methods to catch the trout on streamers with clients.

Store-tied streamers usually did not have enough weight on them to drop through the water column. When I tied streamers with super-heavy dumbbell eyes to reach the desired depth, most of my clients ended up burying the hook in me or themselves. When I switched to sink-tip lines, clients had difficulty casting them. However, I found out that the slower-sinking full-sink lines could be cast by almost anyone with a few pointers, so I went to the full-sinking Type 3 fly line. This allowed a fly with a single tungsten bead or extra-small lead dumbbell eye to be held at the ideal level for the trout.

Designed specifically for the tailwater streams of the Smokies, the Strawberry Blonde quickly earned a reputation as a fish producer in those waters. As anglers gained confidence in the fly, its reputation grew as a consistent fish producer throughout all the watersheds of the region.

I then started playing with different streamers, and went through several variations. I played with everything from bunny strip streamers to regular Woolly Buggers. The trout in the Watauga seemed to key in on tan and light brown better than any other color. I then found some variegated marabou, which unfortunately is no longer on the market; currently I have to make my own. The trout really seemed to like the simplicity of the Woolly Bugger style fly tied with a variegated tail and body.

One day before a guiding trip, I was tying some Strawberry Blondes and I did not have any ³/₁₆-inch gold tungsten beads at home. All I had was metallic red, so I tied some up with the red beads instead of driving back to town to get some gold ones. On the trip the following day, we started with the regular Strawberry Blonde with a gold bead. We were catching a few fish, but over time it got lost to the bottom of the river. All I had left were the Strawberry Blondes I had tied with the red bead.

Still a little skeptical, I tied one on for the client and on the second cast he landed the best trout of the trip. Three of four casts later, he hooked one of the largest brown trout I have ever had a client hook in the United States. Having landed multiple large browns, I can say that if that trout was not 30 inches, it was not an inch. While it ended like most fish stories with the trout going one direction and the angler and fly going the other, it was a battle for a little while. We caught plenty of trout the rest of the day on the red-headed Strawberry Blonde, so I went home wondering if the red bead made a difference or if those trout would have eaten the regular version.

Over the years, I have fished gold-bead and red-bead Strawberry Blondes side by side and can without a doubt say that the red bead makes a big difference on this particular fly. I am not sure whether the trout see it as a sculpin with an egg or just something to eat in their mouth, or if the red bead simply acts as a hot spot and trigger point for the fish. I have tied the fly in various other variegated colors and they all seem to catch a few fish, even the crazy colors like black and white variegations. But the original ginger and brown color proves time and again to be superior.

Tiers can make their own variegated marabou by taking a few fibers of brown, cream, black, and ginger in their fingers and rolling them together until they are blended. The original tail was tied with a product called Jailhouse Marabou from Spirit River, which consisted of four different colors of marabou twisted into a dubbing rope.

Tuckasegee brook trout that ate a red-bead Strawberry Blonde.

Streamer fishing on the Tuckasegee and Watauga Rivers is best when they are under power generation. Anglers will also find a light sink-tip or full-sinking line an added benefit.

Tellico

Tellico
- **Hook:** #8-14 Daiichi 1560 1X-long nymph hook
- **Thread:** Black 6/0 Veevus
- **Body:** Bright yellow floss
- **Rib:** Peacock herl
- **Collar:** Strung brown rooster or hen saddle
- **Back:** Turkey tail feathers
- **Note:** Originally the Tellico was tied using a grouse tail for the back, but most modern tiers use turkey tail because it is more readily available.

The Tellico nymph is often credited to the Reverend Edward Dalstrom from Knoxville, Tennessee. Most of the region's old-school fly tiers disagree with that theory, however, and believe that the fly was originated by fishermen on the Tellico River drainage in Tennessee. Most of the old-timers believe that Dalstrom could read and write unlike many in rural Appalachia. They believe that because of his ability to write down the details that Dalstrom submitted the fly to Ray Bergman, who was the first to write about it and then credited Dalstrom for its creation. Unfortunately, we will never really know the true beginnings of the Tellico.

At age thirteen, I began my professional fly-tying career working for my father and uncle at Dwight and Don's Custom Tackle in Brevard, North Carolina. They sold flies through mail order to retail customers and did a large volume of wholesale to companies like Orvis, George Anderson's Yellowstone Angler, Hunter Banks in Asheville, and other fly shops around the country. As a new young tier, I was given all the orders for Tellico nymphs, Woolly Buggers, and other basic patterns. Tellicos are so popular

The Tellico nymph was the first fly from the Smokies to achieve national attention. There is a lot of debate around its origin, but it was originally featured in Ray Bergman's Trout, *published in 1938. Since then it has been featured in countless articles, magazines, and books.*

and sought after around the park that by the time I reached college, I had tied so many that I refuse to this day to tie them. I am not sure of exactly how many Tellicos I tied over those four or five years, but I know I would go through a thousand pack of size 8 Mustad hooks about every three to four months.

For years a lot of anglers in and around the park wanted their Tellicos tied on straight-eyed Mustad hooks. They would then take the fly and place it behind a number 3 Hildebrandt spinner. This combination proved highly effective at luring large brown trout out of local streams, especially during times of high, off-color water. My father and grandfather often used this technique in low, clear

The golden bullet used by my father and grandfather to locate large trout during the summer months.

Blackburn Tellico (tied by Walter Babb)

water and referred to it as the golden bullet. During the summer months especially, my grandfather would head to the stream and take a spinning reel with him; if the fishing was tough, he would swap reels and put on a Hildebrandt spinner with a Tellico behind it. While the large browns would not often be fooled by the flashy spinner in the lower summer water conditions, they would repeatedly chase it, revealing their location. Once he knew where they were located, he would concentrate on catching them on a fly on future trips.

Over the years, the Tellico has been tweaked, changed, and modified by numerous tiers. The only versions that I have ever encountered that work as well as the original version are the Blackburn Tellico and Beadhead Tellico.

Today, most tiers tie the Tellico with turkey tail for the shell back. The original version was tied from ruffed grouse tail feathers, which were more prominent in the area at the turn of the twentieth century. While the original Tellico rib was a piece of peacock, this material proves to be very fragile and after a couple of fish breaks. I make a chenille-style rope out of the peacock herl, with either a small black wire or black tying thread and two or three pieces of herl. By using this rope instead of one single piece of peacock herl, your flies will be much more durable. I also spray my grouse or turkey feathers with clear Krylon-style spray paint prior to tying. This makes the feathers stiffer and easier to manage during the tying process. Once the fly is completed, I drop a small amount of head cement on the shell back, basically gluing it to the floss body. This will stop the back from busting and breaking apart as quickly, and will also stop the floss body from fraying as much.

Tennessee Wulff

- **Hook:** #10-16 Daiichi 1170 or Mustad 94840
- **Thread:** Black 6/0 Veevus
- **Tail:** Deer hair from back of eastern whitetail
- **Body:** Peacock herl
- **Floss:** Chartreuse UNI-Floss
- **Wings:** White calf tail
- **Hackle:** Brown dry-fly hackle
- **Note:** Some tiers substitute woodchuck for the tail of the fly. White calf body can be substituted for the wings. It is also common to blend grizzly and brown hackle for the Tennessee Wulff.

Tennessee Wulff

The late Lee Wulff's work on hair-wing dry flies led to an entire style of tying and family of flies that would come to bear his name. However, most of the fly designs were already in existence, and he merely switched from a duck quill wing to a hair wing. The Royal Coachman was the inspiration for the Royal Wulff. The same is true for the Tennessee Wulff.

The Tennessee Wulff began life as a fly called the Herbie Werbie. The Herbie Werbie was designed by Herb Harrell, who found his inspiration from a fly called the Gremlin. Once the Royal Wulff and its high-floating properties arrived in the southern Appalachian Mountains, it did not take long for tiers to start incorporating these properties into their popular patterns. Hence the Herbie Werbie's transformation into the Tennessee Wulff.

My introduction to the Tennessee Wulff took place on the West Fork of the Linville River in North Carolina. On a summer trip with my grandfather, we stopped at Hugh's Store in Linville to visit his friend Paul Hughes. Paul was a fellow fly tier and fly fisherman and he sold daily passes to the Linville River. My grandfather purchased us

The Tennessee Wulff is the top attractor pattern of the Smokies. It is especially effective on the smaller drainages where the trout are more opportunistic feeders.

a couple of passes and we headed up the river. I was seventeen at the time and, to my mind, knew all there was to know about fly fishing—I had the newest tippet, best rod, and read all the books.

As we got geared up, my grandfather tied a size 10 Tennessee Wulff onto what looked to be about 20-pound test that he had to trim down at an angle to get it through the fly eye. I laughed and told him that the fly was too big and there was no way any fish would eat it on that tippet. My grandfather told me to take off and fish to my heart's content—he would just fish along behind me and we would meet at 4 o'clock at the club boundary on the West Fork.

I fished through a couple of pools and caught a few trout, all the while with my

Even the smallest of streams in the Smokies that have year-round water flow will have small rainbow and brook trout in the plunge pools waiting on a well-presented dry fly. PHOTO DR PATRICK WILLIAMS

Small rainbows are abundant in park waters and will fall for a Tennessee Wulff, especially in the summer months.

grandfather behind me hollering, "Hey, look at this big one you missed!" or "Look at this one!" By the time we reached the boundary, he had caught double the number of fish than I had and most were larger. So when we moved over to the main part of the river, I gave in and bummed a large, size 10 dry fly from him and tied it on. As we fished, I quickly learned that much of what was taking place was due to the fly because I was catching more fish than before, mainly due to the presentation and placement of the fly.

When tying the Tennessee, Carolina, or Royal Wulff—or any other Wulff for that matter—I have found it easiest to tie in the tail of the fly, then the wings, and then come back and build the body. Tiers will also find that calf tail floats slightly better than calf body hair; however, calf body hair is far easier to work with than calf tail. Also for tails, I prefer the center backstrap portion of the deer hide, as it is darker in nature and tends to flare less.

Texas Piss Ant
- **Hook:** #12-18 Daiichi 1100
- **Thread:** Black 6/0 Veevus
- **Body:** Black dry-fly dubbing
- **Hackle:** Oversized brown hackle, clipped to gap of hook
- **Wing:** White floating poly yarn

Texas Piss Ant

My introduction to the Texas Piss Ant was through my grandfather, who was good friends with Dale and Jerry Hodge and fished in Great Smoky Mountains National Park frequently. The Hodge brothers were especially fond of the Deep Creek and Hazel Creek drainages in the Smokies. Over the years, I have heard countless fishing stories involving my grandfather, father, uncle, and the Hodge brothers. The brothers were fond of fishing black ant patterns in the summertime in the Smokies, but seeing the small ants in the often turbulent waters of the park was difficult. So they started tying the ants in size 10 and 12 and added a white poly wing over the top of the fly to make it easier to find on the water.

On an outing to Hazel Creek with my grandfather one day, the fishing proved to be difficult despite the large population of rainbow trout in the creek. One of the Hodge brothers produced an ant in size 10 from his fly box. After tying on the ant pattern, my grandfather immediately started

Designed by the Hodge brothers of Spruce Pine, North Carolina, the Texas Piss Ant was developed specifically for Hazel Creek. Over the years, the pattern has proven effective around the region and works well during the little black stonefly hatches in late February as well as for Black Caddis and flying ants.

catching trout. His response was that if there was ever an ant that big, it would have to come from Texas, and if it ever bit you, it would bite the piss out of you. From that moment on, the fly was referred to as the Texas Piss Ant.

Over the years, the Texas Piss Ant has been fished from Hazel Creek to South America and all points in between. What was originally tied as an oversized ant has proven an effective pattern for small winter stoneflies, Black Caddis, and just a generally buggy-looking terrestrial that fish are drawn to.

Today I fish the Texas Piss Ant in sizes ranging from 10 to 20. I normally fish a size 10 or 12, but in late summer when fish get extra picky in the low, clear waters in and around the park, I will downsize to a size 16 or 18. I find most success with this fly between late March and mid to late October. In low, clear, late summer conditions, anglers should be fishing the Texas Piss Ant on longer leaders, generally in the 10- to 12-foot range and tapered to 6X tippet. The balance of the year I have not found that the length of the leader makes much difference.

Fishing a Texas Piss Ant on the edge of a leaf line or foam line is an almost guaranteed way to catch a trout. PHOTO DR. PATRICK WILLIAMS

When tying the Texas Piss Ant, tiers should use a fine, light wire hook to aid with flotation. The front and rear sections of the ant are made from a dry-fly-quality dubbing. Oversized hackle that is trimmed down to the gap of the hook is key to the pattern. Once the hackle has been wrapped on the fly and tied off, the fly should be removed from the vise and the hackle clipped to make it the same length as the gap of the hook. By clipping the hackle you are creating blunt ends and making the hackle stiffer in general; both of these conditions result in the fly floating better. The hackle on the top side of the fly needs to be clipped at an angle from lowest in the front to highest in the back; this helps the poly yarn wing lay back over the fly.

The other trick that I commonly apply to this fly is to take a dubbing pick and lightly pick the dubbed body of the fly to make it a little buggier looking and not nice, neat balls of tight dubbing. The reason is that the more I fished the Texas Piss Ant, the more chewed up and rough-looking the fly got and the better it always seemed to fish.

Releasing a Hazel Creek rainbow trout that was caught on a Texas Piss Ant.

Thunderhead
- **Hook:** #12-18 Daiichi 1170 or Mustad 94840
- **Thread:** Black 6/0 Veevus
- **Tail:** Deer tail from back of eastern whitetail
- **Body:** Gray rabbit dubbing with the slightest hue of pink blended into it
- **Wings:** White calf tail
- **Hackle:** Furnace dry-fly hackle
- **Note:** Tiers can substitute white calf body hair for the wings if desired. The calf body wings are a lot neater sitting in a fly bin but do not float quite as well.

Thunderhead

It always amazes me how many flies are created almost simultaneously in various parts of the country. The Thunderhead, which looks a lot like the Adams Wulff, is one such fly, so it is hard to say if one fly creator found inspiration from the other or if they were totally independent events.

The Thunderhead was the creation of the late Fred Hall out of Bryson City, North Carolina, right on the edge of what today is Great Smoky Mountains National Park. Fred was known for tinkering with every fly pattern he ever touched. I believe that he drew inspiration for the Thunderhead from the Adams Wulff. While very similar to the Adams Wulff, the devil is in the details. The original Thunderhead had just a hint of pink to the otherwise gray dubbing of the Adams Wulff, and it made use of deer hair for the tail of the fly. These two changes make perfect sense, since tying materials were very hard to acquire in the southern Appalachian Mountains at the time, and Fred, like most tiers, dyed his own furs for dubbing and made use of local hair and fur as much as possible. I am sure he had some whitetail deer hair lying around that he was using for the tails. Most of the commercially tied

Designed by the late Fred Hall, the Thunderhead is the quintessential dry fly of the Smokies. Its deer hair tail and calf tail wing allow the fly to float high in the area's turbulent waters. The Thunderhead is still a favorite fly of all serious park anglers.

Thunderheads that I see today just make use of an Adams gray dubbing and are nothing more than an Adams Wulff with deer hair substituted for the tail.

My good friend Michael Fields spends more time in the backcountry of the park than any other person I know. Michael says that the Thunderhead is far and away the best-producing fly in his box, especially from late March through mid to late October. He swears that he has seen fish run from one drainage to the next to grab a well-tied Thunderhead. OK, maybe they won't swim from one drainage to the next, but Michael says when the trout in the Smokies refuse to eat any other pattern that he can always catch them on the Thunderhead. It was also a favorite fly of my grandfather's, as he could see its large, bushy white calf tail wings from a long distance. I can remember several trips to the Linville River with him and my father where he only fished the Thunderhead.

I have fished the Thunderhead throughout the park and the surrounding area mainly during the early part of the year when the large, gray mayflies like Quill Gordons are active. It is an exceptionally well-floating and highly visible fly. My grandfather preferred a large, bushy size 12, while Michael says he relies mainly on a size 14 when fishing the streams of the park. I have always found more success in smaller sizes, like a 14 or 16.

When tying a Thunderhead, I typically blend my own dubbing of charcoal gray rabbit with a touch of light pink rabbit. The other key to success with the Thunderhead is the tail. I have found that the deer hair from center back strip of a whitetail deer makes the best tails, as it will not flare and is good and stiff to aid in flotation. A lot of mountain tiers say to use poly yarn when tying Thunderheads. I have tied them with both poly yarn bodies and dubbed bodies and have found the dubbed bodies to be better looking, and longer lasting, and you can tinker with the color a whole lot more.

There is a chocolate version of the Thunderhead as well. I can honestly say that I have known about it most of my life but have never fished the chocolate color, nor do I know of anyone who has.

With its calf tail wings, deer hair tail, and heavy hackle, the Thunderhead was custom built for fishing the turbulent and high-gradient waters so often encountered in the Smokies.

Trina's Tungsten Death Metal

- **Hook:** #12-18 Daiichi 1560
- **Thread:** Veevus 6/0 Black
- **Bead:** Black tungsten
- **Tail:** Pheasant tail
- **Body:** Pheasant tail
- **Thorax:** Peacock
- **Wing case:** Pheasant tail fibers with UV glue top coat
- **Wings:** Pheasant tail

Trina's Tungsten Death Metal

One thing that every fly angler will agree on is how effective a Pheasant Tail Nymph can be. It effectively represents the majority of mayfly nymphs. Over the years of pressure with Pheasant Tails, fish have become a little shy of the gold bead that is often added to the front of the fly for weight. By simply swapping out the gold bead for a black tungsten bead and adding an epoxy back, Adam Trina took the simple and effective Pheasant Tail and turned it into an even more effective fish-catching machine.

I first bumped into the Tungsten Death Metal while fishing with my good friend Gonzalo Flego in San Martín de los Andes,

Argentina. During a slow period in the day, we started dropping the fly below a Chubby Chernobyl and catching a lot of fish on it. I immediately noticed how close to a Pheasant Tail the fly was and how the dark bead did not seem to spook the fish as much.

On my return to the mountains of Western North Carolina and East Tennessee, I called the guys at Montana Fly Company and got some of the flies into the bins of the shop. The Davidson River, as with most streams in the Smokies, sees an extreme amount of angling pressure. While guiding I have seen clients make a drift with a gold bead Pheasant Tail and the fish separate

Trina's Tungsten Death Metal (above fly tied by Montana Fly Company) is representative of the majority of mayfly nymphs in the region's streams. With its heavy tungsten bead and slim cylindrical body this fly will get deep quick, and it produces strikes when a normal Pheasant Tail Nymph will not.

as the fly approaches them; they let the fly wash by and then move right back into the feeding lanes they were in as if the fly was never there. Yet flies with no bead or with a dark-colored bead do not seem to spook the same fish.

This spooky behavior could be due to the fact that I typically sell anywhere from eighty to ninety dozen size 14 gold bead Pheasant Tails annually through the shop. That is 960 to 1,080 identical gold bead flies that get fished on the same 12 miles of river. Those trout could tell you the name of the person that produced the bead and if they are left- or right-handed. For years I carried a black or brown Sharpie with me while guiding and colored my gold beads to be anything except gold. Once I discovered the Tungsten Death Metal, I started guiding with it exclusively instead of a Pheasant Tail. Fish do not spook away from the dark bead, and it still has a Pheasant Tail look and feel to it.

Southern Appalachian trout for the most part are very opportunistic feeders, with the exception of a couple of streams. And for most patterns I have never really found that size matters nearly as much as the presentation of the fly. However, most of our mayfly larvae in the southern Appalachians are pretty small, especially on rivers like the Davidson, South Holsten, Watauga, and other highly pressured streams in the region. Due to this pressure, I tend to fish this pattern in smaller sizes than I would typically be inclined to use. As for sizes, I typically sell more size 14 than anything (mainly because that is an easy size to tie on); however, I typically fish sizes 16 to 20, as I think those size nymphs do a better job at representing the size of the mayfly larvae that are typically found in the area.

As for tying the Tungsten Death Metal, I tie a couple dozen of them and line them up, then apply the UV resin to the back of the flies and set the glue with a UV light. I also tend to tie my Tungsten Death Metals as sparsely as I can. The sparsely tied flies look more realistic in the water and they also sink quicker, which keeps them down in the strike zone longer.

Lindsay Rutland high-stick nymphing a Tungsten Death Metal along undercut rocks. High-sticking and Czech nymphing are both highly productive ways to fish in the region.
PHOTO DAVID CANNON

Trude

Carter Harrison developed the Trude as a wet fly while living in Chicago around the turn of the twentieth century. In 1908, while fishing in Idaho, he added a large hair wing and a body fashioned from red carpet as a joke. What started as a joke has proven to be the basis for countless fly patterns and one of the best trout-producing flies of all time.

I am not sure if the trout take the Trude for a caddis, stonefly, or grasshopper or just think it is flashy and might taste good. For fishing in and around Great Smoky Mountains National Park, I prefer a Royal or lime-colored Trude. The Lime Trude tends to be most effective when the Yellow Sallies or Green Sallies are active. The Royal Trude is a great searching pattern on all the waters of the park, and when fishing on some of the small brook trout waters you may have to hide behind a tree to tie it on because it is so effective. I tend to use the Royal Trude in the summer months through early fall until we have a heavy frost that reduces the number of active terrestrials along the stream bank. The Royal Trude seems to excel when you cast along the bank under overhanging laurel and sycamore limbs. Some of the old-timers tell me they think the trout take it for an ant; I personally think that it looks buggy

The Lime Trude is an excellent choice for anglers fishing the Little Green Stonefly hatch.

and fish eat it thinking it is just a large insect that fell out of a tree.

One of my most memorable experiences with a Royal Trude came on the Oconaluftee River near the Toe String Bridge. My father and I were fishing up the river, and I was using a Trude. I don't really recall what my father was using, but the fish were readily taking both flies and, as usual, we were alternating turns fishing as we went up the river. He cast under an overhanging limb and a fish rose and took his fly, and in some strange act of nature he missed the fish and got hung on a limb. As I laughed at his missed fish I told him not worry, that I would show him how to catch the fish. I made a cast to the fish and my line went right over the limb he was hung on, and the fly stopped about 2 inches above the surface of the water. No sooner had the fly come to rest above the water's surface than a very large rainbow trout rocketed from the depths and inhaled the fly as it dangled above the water. This left me in a real pickle, as I was hooked to a really nice fish but wound up in not only a laurel limb but now also my father's fly line. Then the limb broke

Flashy attractors like the Royal Trude are a great choice when fishing for true southern strain brook trout.

Searching for brook trout high in the Smoky Mountains. PHOTO DR. PATRICK WILLIAMS

off and I came tight on the fish, only to have my line break. My father just laughed and said that's what I got for laughing at him.

When tying a Trude for the park region, I highly recommend a calf tail wing to aid in the flotation of the fly. Again, I have seen them tied from several different types of synthetic material, and none of them seem to float as well as the calf tail. I have also used calf body hair for the wings, which stacks nice and neat and looks better than the calf tail but again is not quite as buoyant.

Over the years, I have played with several different colors and variations of the Trude. I have often thought that a yellow-bodied Trude would work exceptionally well in the park and have tried it several times, but have never found it to produce fish as well as some of the other yellow-based fly patterns in this book.

Tungsten Jig Pheasant Tail

Fly tiers are a lot like deer hunters—always on the hunt for something they can incorporate into their next fly or something that may help them catch one more fish than their buddy. How else can you explain a grown man sifting through the thousands of skeins of yarn at Hobby Lobby? Hooks are no exception to the tinkering. Over the years, we have bent and modified hooks countless ways to make a better or more realistic fly.

Every angler that fishes with conventional gear knows how powerful a tool a jig is. We started tying on larger-size jig hooks over the years for a number of reasons, the key reason being you don't dull your hook point by dragging on rocks and you seem to get a better hookup. The first jig flies were tied on small number 8 jig hooks used for crappie and other panfish. Then we started bending the 90-degree bend out to get beads to slide up on the bend of the hook. Then came bead modifications to fit easier on the jig hook. Today as a fly tier you have an endless supply of jig-style hooks, all pre-bent to different angles for different applications.

With a slim profile and large tungsten bead head, the Tungsten Jig Pheasant Tail will get to the bottom and hold there. The Pheasant Tail jig also successfully replicates over 70 percent of all mayfly nymphs.

A lot of flies have been adapted to jig hooks, but one of the first was the Pheasant Tail, as it effectively represents the majority of the mayfly nymphs. The beauty of the jig-style fly and especially the Pheasant Tail in the Smokies is that it features a heavy tungsten head and a small cylindrical body, which allows the fly to sink quickly through the turbulent waters and reach the bottom with ease. Once on the bottom it can bounce and drag along without many hang-ups, all while keeping your hook away from the rocks.

I was an early adopter of the jig-style Pheasant Tail. While I can't speak to a specific story or event that I can remember about fishing the Jig Pheasant Tail, I can say that I have acquired so much confidence in the fly that it will often be one of the first two or three flies I fish at any location. Most of the time, I find myself starting and ending with a Jig Pheasant Tail tied somewhere in my bite of flies. I will also say that the heavier, the better, so that it can get to the bottom and stay there. I have not found success with jig-style nymphs being drifted partway through the water column.

There are countless ways to modify the Jig Pheasant Tail. The easiest and most common variations are color-based, with black and olive dyed pheasant tail commonly being substituted for the body. One of the more recent variations comes from the exploding popularity of the Euro nymphing revolution of adding a hot spot (trigger point) of some UV-colored dubbing just behind the bead. I also find myself tying and fishing either a rubber leg or soft-hackle version of the fly.

When tying Jig Pheasant Tails for my personal use, I often use two different beads. One bead should be normally sized to the hook you are using, but for fishing in stronger current or in higher water flows I will tie some of the flies with a bead that is one size larger than normal for the hook. I also recommend making the body thin and wispy, as I have found that to produce better than a large, bulky body. You can use just about any bead color, but I prefer black for highly pressured streams and standard gold for streams that are not heavily pressured. As for the hot spot, I have tried several colors and always end back at red for the Pheasant Tail.

Nymphing on the transition lines with a Tungsten Jig Pheasant Tail is a guaranteed way to catch some trout.

Woolly Bugger (Black)

- **Hook:** #2-16 Daiichi 2220 or Mustad 79580
- **Thread:** Black 6/0 Veevus
- **Tail:** Black strung marabou
- **Body:** Black chenille (medium)
- **Hackle:** Webby black saddle hackle or schlappen
- **Rib:** Wire, color to match body (brassie)
- **Note:** Woolly Buggers can be tied in hundreds of colors; the best colors for the Smokies, in addition to black, are white, olive, and peacock.

Woolly Bugger

Of all the flies on the market, and there are thousands of them these days, the Woolly Bugger, the Clouser, and the Deceiver are the only three patterns that I know of that transcend all species. Of these three, it would be a toss-up as to whether the Clouser or Woolly Bugger is the GOAT.

My introduction to the Woolly Bugger came at the age of thirteen. My father and uncle were headed to Alaska, and I was tasked with helping tie flies for them. They were in need of Egg-Sucking Buggers and Black Woolly Buggers for use on their upcoming trip, and

I got to noticing how much the Black Woolly Bugger looked like a black salamander. So I tied up some size 4 and 6 Black Woolly Buggers to try in the local streams around the park. During my early years of fishing with my grandfather, trout were a food source for him, and I had to be pretty dang quick to release one without his noticing and it ending up on his dinner table. I never helped him clean a large trout (over 16 inches) in the summertime that did not have at least one if not multiple salamanders in its belly. I knew with Dad headed to Alaska that my fishing

The Black Woolly Bugger is a great representation of the many hellgrammites found in the Smokies, and it can also represent a salamander or dark-colored dace in larger sizes. Every angler should have a few different-colored Woolly Buggers in assorted sizes in their box.

partner for the next couple of weeks would be my grandfather.

A couple of days later, we were headed to the Oconaluftee River. As we arrived at the river, it began raining and the river slowly rose all day. In the high, dark-colored water the Woolly Bugger really showed its potential. By the end of the day, my grandfather had even been converted from his tried-and-true Bitch Creek Nymph to a Black Woolly Bugger.

Since those early days, I have fished a Woolly Bugger in about every color that you can dream up and in about any size that you can find a hook. To this day, believe that a properly tied size 4 or 6 Black Woolly Bugger is one of the best salamander imitations that an angler heading into Great Smoky Mountains National Park can have in their fly box. I often see anglers convinced that a trout will not eat a fly bigger than a size 8

The Peacock Herl Woolly Bugger offers a slightly different color scheme for the trout. The natural iridescent shine of the peacock herl draws strikes from even the most finicky fish.

The long, deep pools of the Oconaluftee, Little, Tuck, Watauga, Toe, and other larger rivers of the region are perfect for those anglers looking for a streamer fix.

in our area. While you will catch a lot of fish on the smaller Buggers, I am convinced that the big trout love big, fat salamanders and I often fish Woolly Buggers up to a size 2.

When tying Woolly Buggers, I see a lot of companies and tiers clip the marabou straight at the desired tail length. This totally kills the swimming action of the tail! To tie the best swimming, most effective Buggers, start with extra-select marabou that you have to clip from the stem. The so-called Woolly Bugger marabou is short and has thin stems embedded in it that if not removed will kill the action of the fly. Thinner tails also tend to swim better than thick tails.

Over the years, I have seen lots of variations including bead and cone heads, the addition of Flashabou and Krystal Flash, rubber legs, etc. In all of my fishing and travels, I have realized that I can narrow my Woolly Bugger selection down to three necessary colors: black, olive, and white. You can add flash and rubber legs to dress them up a little if you'd like. I have also found in heavily pressured streams that a purple or peacock herl body under the black hackle will work when basic black may get refused.

Yallar Hammer Dry Fly

- **Hook:** #10-16 Daiichi 1170 or Mustad 94840
- **Thread:** Uni Thread 6/0 bright yellow
- **Tail:** Light ginger hackle fibers
- **Body:** Bright yellow floss palmered with imitation Yallar Hammer feather
- **Wings:** Barred wood duck flank
- **Hackle:** Light ginger

Yallar Hammer Dry Fly

I am not sure who created the dry-fly version of the Yallar Hammer. It, like the other versions of the Yallar Hammer, has multiple variations. Regardless of which tier first started tinkering with the Yallar Hammer, they understood the importance that the bright-colored flicker feather played in the fly. It is believed that the dry version was created to imitate the Little Yellow Stonefly that is so prevalent in the steams of Great Smoky Mountains National Park. While tied similar to a Catskill pattern, the dry version of the Yallar Hammer is hackled heavier, more in the style of a Wulff or Humpy than a Cahill.

When the dry-fly version of the Yallar Hammer was being designed, quality tying materials were very difficult to obtain in the rural Appalachian Mountains. Quality materials were only available by mail order until the mid-1970s, when Dwight and Don Howell opened Dwight and Don's Custom Tackle and stocked quality materials for the local tiers to purchase. Until this point, materials were what you could find around the house or yard or via mail order, if you had the money, from a tying house in a different state. This explains the simple nature of the Yallar Hammer Dry Fly. The underbody can

The Yallar Hammer Dry Fly has survived decades by being a proven fish catcher. It can be equally effective when fished during a Yellow Drake hatch as it is during a Yellow Sally hatch. It is also highly effective as a searching pattern for brook trout.

be produced from yellow floss, or in most cases yellow thread. The feather over the yellow body is typically a secondary or tertiary wing feather, which is smaller and softer in nature than the primary feathers. The tier would then clip the feather barbs to make a tapered body. The ginger hackle was probably plucked from a ginger-colored chicken in the yard, and the wood duck plumage for the wings was probably taken from ducks harvested from nearby rivers for food.

My uncle, Dwight Howell, was far more of dry-fly angler than my father. I can remember many trips into the Smoky Mountains with him in early June when he and I would fish nothing but Yallar Hammer Dry Flies, especially on the Oconaluftee and Cataloochee system streams. Walking in on the Bradley Fork was always a great day of dry-fly fishing. The single largest brook trout I ever caught was on the Bradley Fork with Uncle Dwight. Any native brook trout in the Southeast that is bigger than 7 inches is a monster—that brookie was pushing 15 inches! I had never seen a true southern strain brook trout of that size before that day and have not seen one since. I still fish

that area with the enthusiasm of a teenager, hoping that he or some other long-lost brookie is lurking around the area looking for a tasty Yallar Hammer for breakfast.

Yallar Hammer feathers are tricky to tie with. The best way to make the feathers manageable for tying is to soak them in a cup of room-temperature water for 20 to 30 minutes prior to tying. This will make the feathers very soft and pliable, and they can be easily manipulated around a hook. You will also want to find the curve in the feather and remove the barbs from the underside of the curve; this allows the stem to lie flat on the hook or underbody. Make sure that the feather is tied in tip first so that when you palmer the feather, the fly is wider at the front than at the back. Once you have the Yallar Hammer feather palmered forward and tied off, use a pair of sharp scissors to trim the barbs of the feather to form a tapered body that is smallest at the tail and larger as you move forward. The original underbody was tied out of yellow floss; however, for the last several years I have been building my underbodies out of bright yellow thread, which is quicker and easier.

Author Kevin Howell still searching for the offspring of the monster brook trout that took a Yallar Hammer Dry Fly when he was a teenager.
PHOTO DAVID CANNON

Yallar Hammer Nymph
- **Hook:** #8-12 Daiichi 1710 or Mustad 9671
- **Thread:** Red 70-denier Ultra Thread
- **Tail:** Brown feather barbs
- **Body:** Bright yellow floss palmered with imitation feathers
- **Wing case:** Turkey tail
- **Thorax:** Yellow chenille
- **Hackle:** Brown soft hackle
- **Underbody:** lead wire .010–.030 diameter

Yallar Hammer Nymph

Like the other two versions of the Yallar Hammer, it is difficult to discern who created the original nymph version. Over the years, a number of tiers have created a multitude of slightly different variations, including yours truly.

It is a common belief that the Yallar Hammer Nymph was originally created to replicate the nymphs of the Golden and Little Yellow Stoneflies that are so common in the area. The other popular belief is that it was created to replicate a yellow jacket, which for some strange reason trout seem to find tasty. I typically just find yellow jackets painful and annoying as I am trying to bust through brush to get to the stream to fish.

I can't say that I have ever had a huge amount of success with the Yallar Hammer Nymph. I think this is mainly due to the fact that I have not spent much time at all with it tied onto the end of my line. I do have plenty of clients—and I mean plenty—who are fanatics about the Yallar Hammer Nymph and its fish-catching power. I have,

One of the most famous of flies of the Great Smoky Mountains is the Yallar Hammer Nymph, which is as effective today as it was a hundred years ago.

however, had good success with a version that I stumbled upon by accident at the tying vise one day. While tying some beaded soft hackles, I got to looking at the stuff on my tying desk and noticed I had Yallar Hammer feathers soaking in a cup of water, left over from a tying session the day before. I also had some rubber legs from tying Kevin's Stonefly lying around, so as most tiers do, I started to play around and mix materials and shapes together until I had something I thought might work.

Turns out the Improved Yallar Hammer Nymph has been a very successful variation. Most of my friends that swear by the Yallar Hammer Nymph say that it fishes the best from late April through early August, and I have found that to be true for the Improved Yallar Hammer as well. Most anglers prefer a size 8 or 10 for the original nymph version, but I have found a size 12 or 14 works best for the Improved Yallar Hammer.

When it comes to tying the Yallar Hammer Nymph, there are a couple things to consider. It does have a lead underbody, and you will need to cover the body with floss

The Improved Yallar Hammer Nymph fishes well as a Yellow Sally nymph and can also be tied in a chocolate color.

or thread. Secondly, as stated in the Yellow Hammer Dry Fly chapter, Yallar Hammer feathers are tricky to tie with. The best way to make the feathers manageable for tying is to soak them in a cup of room-temperature water for 20 to 30 minutes prior to tying. This will make the feathers very soft and pliable, and they can be easily manipulated around a hook. You will also want to find the curve in the feather and remove the barbs from the underside of the curve; this allows the stem to lie flat on the hook or underbody. Make sure that the feather is tied in tip first so that when you palmer the feather, the fly is wider at the front than at the back. Once you have the Yallar Hammer feather palmered forward and tied off, use a pair of sharp scissors to trim the barbs of the feather to form a tapered body that is smallest at the tail and larger as you move forward. The original underbody was tied out of yellow floss; however, for the last several years I have been building my underbodies out of bright yellow thread, which is quicker and easier.

For the Improved Yallar Hammer Nymph, I tie the small brown rubber legs onto the front of the hook prior to sliding the bead on the hook. The shell back is formed by either epoxy over the turkey tail wing case or UV glue. The UV glue is quicker and neater; however, I have found that 5-minute epoxy really stands up to the test of time. If you use 5-minute epoxy, you will have to rotate the fly to keep the epoxy from sagging and running to one side. I have tied the Improved Yallar Hammer on a regular straight-shank nymph hook but have found that it is far more effective when tied on a curved scud hook.

Yallar Hammer Nymphs are especially effective in the spring when the dogwoods are blooming.
PHOTO DAVID CANNON

Yallar Hammer Original

Yallar Hammer Original
- **Hook:** #8-12 Daiichi 1710 or Mustad 9671
- **Thread:** Black Veevus PB 140 denier or 3/0 black Uni-Thread
- **Wire:** Lead wire (.020)
- **Tail:** Golden pheasant tippet
- **Body:** Black or orange floss or wool
- **Hackle:** Imitation Yallar Hammer feather palmered through the body

No one is exactly sure who tied or fished the original Yallar Hammer. It is widely believed that it was probably a Cherokee Indian who brought down a yellow-shafted flicker with his blowgun, then took the brightly colored feathers and lashed them to a deer bone hook with a piece of rawhide. Thus was born the most iconic of all southern trout flies.

The original version of the Yallar Hammer was nothing more than a feather wrapped around a hook. It is important to note that the feather was tied in a reverse palmer style so that the barbs of the feather faced forward toward the hook point. The fly was fished by allowing it to float downstream and then twitched back upstream. This causes the feather to collapse back on the hook when twitched and then spring

The most iconic of all southern Appalachian trout flies, the original Yallar Hammer has been fished in the waters of the Smokies for over two hundred years. Originally designed to be floated downstream and slowly twitched back upstream, anglers will find this fly to be as effective today as when it was originally created.

forward when at rest. Due to the nature of the flicker feather, which is iridescent black on one side and bright yellow on the other, the fly looks alive and switches from black to yellow and back to black.

While this technique started with the Cherokee, it was quickly adopted by the early settlers of area that is now Great Smoky Mountains National Park and proved deadly on the region's native brook trout population. I have tried this technique and found success with it. However, there is a learning curve: Some strikes are vicious, and if an angler has a tight line in hand, he will be left without a fly on the end of the line. Also, this technique works best when you can allow the fly to drift under a cutbank or log. In addition, with all the fishing pressure our streams receive, I have relegated this technique to times of higher water flows and off-color or stained water. The darker-stained water helps mask your approach to the wary fish.

Since the northern yellow-shafted flicker is considered a threatened species, you can no longer use or possess their feathers without a permit from the US Fish and Wildlife Service. Over the years, many tiers, including myself, have tried to duplicate the

Orange Yallar Hammer

feather of the northern flicker. Through lots of experimentation I have found that dyed dove, quail, and Hungarian partridge feathers make the best substitute, even though there is no way to get the total black iridescent sheen on one side and bright yellow on the other that you find on flicker feathers. Just be sure that you have legally harvested the feathers or have purchased them from a reputable retailer and that you are not in violation of the Federal Migratory Bird Act.

While this is a simple pattern to tie, Yallar Hammer or substitute Yallar Hammer feathers are tricky to tie with. Many articles have been written about taking a razor blade and splitting the shaft of the feather to make it more manageable. This process was likely devised by a doctor who needed some business in stitching up fingers that have been sliced open by razor blades. The best way to make the feathers manageable for tying is to soak them in cup of room-temperature water for 20 to 30 minutes prior to tying. This will make the feathers very soft and pliable, and they can be easily manipulated around a hook. You will also want to find the curve in the feather and remove the barbs from the underside of the curve; this allows the stem to lie flat on the hook or underbody. Make sure that the feather is tied in tip first so that when you palmer the feather, the fly is wider at the front than at the back. Be sure to construct this pattern with 3/0 or 140-denier thread, as smaller threads do not bind the stiff feather down as well.

You will see several variations of the original Yallar Hammer; some will have orange, yellow, or black dubbing (originally rag wool) under the palmered hackle, while others feature a golden pheasant tippet for the tail. Keep in mind that the original pattern was just a feather and a hook.

Yellow Irresistible
- **Hook:** #10-16 Daiichi 1170
- **Thread:** Black 6/0 Veevus
- **Tail:** Eastern whitetail deer from center of back
- **Body:** Bright yellow deer belly hair, spun and clipped
- **Wing:** Grizzly hackle tips from a grizzly hen neck
- **Hackle:** Brown and grizzly Whiting Dry Fly Hackle, mixed

Yellow Irresistible

The one constant in Great Smoky Mountains National Park in the summertime, other than the crowds, is the almost daily thunderstorms. Some days these storms are short-lived and only add a small amount of water to the river. Other days these storms may dump as much as 2 inches of rain in a drainage before dissipating. All of this rain conditions the trout—they know that if they lie and wait that every afternoon the river will rise and flush crayfish, minnows, darts, and salamanders to them for a buffet-style feast. This daily phenomenon will leave the trout stuffed, not wanting to feed, and oftentimes anglers scratching their head about how to fool the wary trout.

As a teenager, I would spend as much time as possible fishing with my grandfather in the summertime. I would go spend a week or two with him and my grandmother under the pretense of helping him trim and shape his Christmas trees. However, that usually lasted about a half a day before he hired someone else to trim his trees and he

During rain events the trout of the Smokies gorge themselves with salamanders and crayfish, often to the point of being stuffed and not wanting to feed. The Yellow Irresistible will often draw a strike in these times of high, clear water and trout with full bellies, kind of like eating apple pie after Thanksgiving dinner.

and I would head to the local streams and ponds of Western North Carolina and Great Smoky Mountains National Park. It was here where he showed me how to fool the picky, summertime, post-rainfall trout. He had a very specific technique which I have never seen anyone other than my father, uncle, and grandfather and a few of their really close friends use.

The technique was the use of the Yellow Irresistible. I am not sure where my grandfather learned about the Yellow Irresistible, but I know that my father and uncle, and later myself, would tie them for him. When I first saw the pattern, it had grizzly hackle tips for wings, though in later years my grandfather would have us tie them with white calf tail wings so that he could see them better. I never noticed that one version outperformed the other.

Oftentimes we would not leave the house until the rains had started or were completely done for the afternoon—I don't think

The Yellow Irresistible works best when the stream has been high for days and the fish have fed heavily and are starting to get picky on streamers and large nymph patterns.
PHOTO DAVID CANNON

my grandfather liked getting soaking wet. As the river came up, we would fish large nymphs and streamers until the river crested and started to recede. Once this happened, most of the streams in and around the park would have a slight tea color to them. Often as the river crested and started to fall back to its normal level or if we started the morning after a really heavy rain the evening before, this was when the fish would be at their pickiest. My grandfather would take his nymph or streamer off and replace it with a size 10 or 12 Yellow Irresistible. He would still be using a heavier-than-normal tippet, usually about a 4X (6-pound test). He would then proceed to catch trout where I had just fished with a nymph or streamer. His theory was that the trout had fed heavily on the large forage and were lying there full, and that his little yellow fly was somehow viewed as dessert. He said there was always room for some ice cream to clean the palate and slide into all the crevices. To this day I still use this technique and it proves highly effective when trout have been feeding heavily during rain events and the river is falling and has a slight stain to it.

I have never seen a Yellow Irresistible tied for sale in any shop, so you are going to have to tie this pattern yourself or contract someone to tie it for you. When tying the Yellow Irresistible, tiers should source the best dyed deer belly hair that they can find—this will make spinning the body much easier. Also, a good set or razor scissors will help with trimming the body to the size and shape that you want. I have always seen the body a little more exaggerated (dramatic taper) than most dry-fly bodies.

Yellow Mayfly
- **Hook:** #10-18 Daiichi 1170
- **Thread:** Light Cahill 6/0 UNI-Thread
- **Tail:** Light Cahill hackle barbs
- **Body:** Creamy yellow rabbit dubbing
- **Wing:** Lemon barred wood duck
- **Hackle:** Golden straw Whiting Dry Fly Hackle

Yellow Mayfly

Some of my best and most memorable fly-fishing experiences as a teenager revolved around the yellow mayfly (aka yellow drake). Once the Yellow Mayflies started coming off in late April or early May, my father, uncle, and I would spend six out of seven nights a week for nearly a month fishing the Yellow Fly hatch, as they called it. The hatch would not get started until around 8:00 p.m., so we would leave the house around 6 and fish various stretches of the river to have us in position at the long, flat slicks just before or right as the drakes started popping off. These were large size 10 or 12 mayflies, and they would have every trout in the river looking up.

I can remember standing at the intake hole for the Pisgah Fish Hatchery and catching multiple 20-inch trout in an evening, all on dries. I can also remember other spots where I could stand in my foot tracks and land over twenty-five trout on dries in less than an hour. The darker it got, the better the fishing got; I vividly remember trying to tie flies on by holding them up to the moon and trying to shove 3X tippets through the eye of the fly. We would often return home after 11:00 p.m., all geared up to do it again the next evening.

While the Yellow Mayfly is often confused with the Light Cahill, it has a heavier hackle for the turbulent waters of the Smokies as well as a brighter yellow body than a Cahill.

In the spring of 1997, a couple of months after I married my wonderful wife, my buddy John and I fished the hatch long after sunset. My wife and his, not being accustomed to this phenomenon, thought we should have been home shortly after dark. They called my mother, who told them not to worry, we would be home eventually. Well, when 10:30 p.m. rolled around and we still weren't home, Mellissa and Danette decided that something dreadful had happened, so they started called calling the sheriff's office and rescue squad. We arrived home around 11, just as they were gearing up for a full-on search-and-rescue operation in Pisgah National Forest for John and me. After a severe tongue-lashing from our wives, we headed back out the next night for the Yellow Drake hatch once again.

A lot of anglers confuse this fly with the Light Cahill pattern, which is easy to do at first glance. I feel certain they do share some family lineage; however, the Yellow Mayfly has a much brighter yellow tint to the body and is generally tied in larger sizes. The original version of the Yellow Mayfly was tied with a spun fur body; however, spun fur is very hard to find on the market these days. The spun fur was also not very durable and tended to absorb water very badly once in the mouth of a trout. Over the years, my father and I both played with various dubbing blends to make the fly a little more durable. After countless variations, I have found that bright yellow rabbit dubbing blended with cream rabbit dubbing in equal amounts makes the best bodies and dubbing for the Yellow Mayfly.

The original version of this fly, as taught to me by my father, who tied thousands of them annually, had split wings fashioned from lemon barred wood duck or mallard flank dyed to a wood duck color. I have also tied the fly with white calf tail wings, which make it more visible to the angler in low-light conditions. My favorite variation is to tie this pattern in a parachute form. If you find spun fur available on the market and decide to use it, be sure to keep the fur twisted in the same direction that it comes off the spool. Otherwise, it will simply unravel with the first couple of fish.

Larger pools with silty bottoms are the best areas for fishing the Yellow Drake hatch. Don't expect much activity until the last hour of daylight. The peak of the hatch will be from the beginning of May to the end of June, depending on stream elevation and location.
PHOTO DAVID CANNON

Yellow Sally
- **Hook:** #12-18 Daiichi 1170
- **Thread:** Bright yellow 6/0 UNI-Thread
- **Body:** Bright yellow rabbit dubbing
- **Wing:** Yearling or bull elk
- **Hackle:** Golden straw Whiting Dry Fly Hackle
- **Note:** Some tiers place a red egg sac on the back of the body.

Yellow Sally

The Little Yellow Stonefly (aka Yellow Sally) is a very common insect in and around the streams of Great Smoky Mountains National Park. Little Yellow Stoneflies can be hatching in the park's waters as early as April and as late as September. They tend to be most active in the early mornings, especially in the summer months after a cooling rain the night prior. Anglers should also take note that the Great Smoky Mountains region is also home to a little stonefly that when it hatches looks just like the Yellow Stone but is bright (almost chartreuse) green. It too hatches during the summer months.

My first encounter with little yellow stoneflies was while I was fishing the yellow mayfly (yellow drake) hatches during my teenage years. These hatches occurred during May, when it seemed that every hatching insect was bright yellow in nature. It was not until I started guiding in the late 1980s that I discovered that these insects were a major food source for several months of the year.

In 2006, while guiding a client named Jim on the Davidson River, I had a morning with

The Yellow Sally is the most prolific of all the hatches in the Smokies. Not only are they available in May and June, but anglers will also encounter smaller hatches of the insect throughout the summer months, especially following light summer rains.

the Yellow Sally that I will never forget. It was Memorial Day, and I was dreading the trip because I knew how crowded the forest was going to be. We met at the shop at 6:00 a.m. and went fishing on the upper Davidson through Horse Cove. By 6:30, as we approached the Roving Indian Joe Hole, I noticed some Sallies starting to hatch and a large trout sipping flies near the bank. After rerigging Jim to a Yellow Sally, he made a cast (not particularly a good one either) and the fish took the fly on the first drift. He landed a nice 21-inch rainbow trout, and I thought, wow, that was nice bonus fish for the morning. As we rounded the bend, I noticed another nice fish rising and again Jim's cast was close, but by no means did the fly land where it should have. But the fish left its feeding lane and took the Yellow Sally on the first drift. This time Jim landed a 19-inch brown trout. I thought, well, that is our day—we will only catch a couple of dinks from here on out.

As we approached the Sycamore Hole, the Sallies had stopped hatching except for a sporadic stone here or there, but the trout did not seem to mind. By the time that we reached the Hatchery Flat, Jim had landed five rainbows between 19 and 23 inches and one 19-inch brown, not to mention countless 10- to 15-inch trout, all on a Yellow Sally. As we drove back to the shop, Jim, who was relatively new to fly fishing, looked at me and said, "I really thought the fishing would be better." I had to explain to him that he had just experienced what would probably be the most epic day of dry-fly fishing in his fly-fishing career.

There are countless Yellow Sally patterns available on the market. Over the years, I have fished with the majority of them and can tell you that for the area in and around Great Smoky Mountains National Park, I look for a pattern that has either a heavy hackle or a lot of deer or elk hair in it to help it float in the turbulent waters around the park. For the green version, there is no stock pattern offered, so anglers will have to tie their own. I tie the same pattern as the Yellow Sally but in a bright green color.

Regardless of how well you tie your Yellow Sally pattern, it is always difficult to compete with the real thing.
PHOTO DAVID CANNON

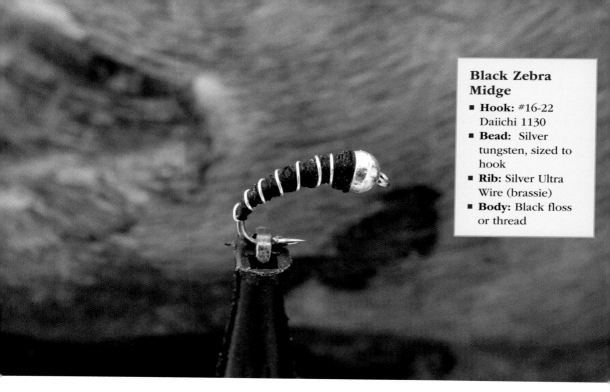

Black Zebra Midge
- **Hook:** #16-22 Daiichi 1130
- **Bead:** Silver tungsten, sized to hook
- **Rib:** Silver Ultra Wire (brassie)
- **Body:** Black floss or thread

Zebra Midge

The Zebra Midge was developed by Lee's Ferry, Arizona, guide Ted Welling as a midge pupa. Ted probably did not think that his fly would end up in the box of every trout guide in the world, but it did. While not originally developed for use in the Great Smoky Mountains area, the fly quickly found a home in the box of every serious southern Appalachian angler.

My first introduction to the Zebra Midge was from the guys at Madison River Fishing Company in Ennis, Montana. I was fishing the Madison below Ennis Lake, and guy behind the counter at MRFC told me the new fly had been producing a lot of fish. So I purchased a couple of Zebra Midges and headed down the river. The flies seemed to produce fish almost instantly.

Upon my return to Pisgah Forest and the streams of the Smokies, I was anxious to try my new fly discovery. I was guiding a trip on the upper Davidson River near the Pisgah Fish Hatchery; it was late fall, and nothing really seemed to be producing many fish. Looking through my box, I saw the Zebra Midge and decided to give it a shot. On the first cast my client was hooked up on a nice rainbow. For the next couple of hours

The Black Zebra Midge is not only a great midge representation but also an important caddis imitation. The Zebra Midge will catch fish year-round but will really shine from mid-November through mid-March when the Black Caddis begin to hatch.

we caught several fish, and eventually both of the Zebra Midges that I had had been depleted or at least sacrificed to the overhanging mountain laurel. I returned home and tied up some Zebra Midges with both brass and tungsten beads and in assorted colors. Over the next few weeks, I came to have a lot of trust in the power of the Zebra Midge.

A few years later, I had a guide working for me that when guiding would always start every trip with a Zebra Midge tied on to the end of the line. There were far more days that he came back to the shop with a Zebra Midge still tied on than days when he came home with a different pattern on his line.

I believe that the Zebra Midge's effectiveness is derived from the fact that it not only replicates a midge pupa but also numerous types of caddis. The other distinct advantage of the Zebra Midge comes from its small cylindrical shape and heavy tungsten bead, which allow it to cut through the current and get deep in the strike zone quickly.

Today, Zebra Midges come in lots of sizes and colors. It is common to encounter red, brown, purple, and even two-tone color patterns. I have also seen the pattern modified by adding one or two strands of pearl Krystal Flash as a tail on the fly. A fly commonly known as the Jerry Garcia is nothing more than a Zebra Midge ribbed with chartreuse and pink thread. With all of the variations and adaptations of this fly, I still find the Black Zebra Midge with a silver wire rib and a matching silver tungsten bead is far and away the best producer, followed closely by a red-bodied Zebra with silver wire and a silver bead.

Another variation to the Zebra Midge is to tie the fly with a glass bead, which makes for a great pattern in low water. This variation also serves well as a floating nymph when trout are feeding on midges just below the surface.

While the Zebra Midge is probably the most basic of all flies to tie, I have found that tying the body with a flat-lying thread like Ultra Thread makes the neatest fly. I have also been tying Zebra Midges with Veevus Body Quill, which gives the fly a nice little sparkle effect. As for the best sizes, I typically fish a size 16 to 22, with 18 being my go-to size.

While Zebra Midges are effective year-round, they are especially effective in the winter months.
PHOTO J. E. B. HALL

Zirdle Bug

Black Zirdle Bug
- **Hook:** #4-12 Daiichi 2220
- **Thread:** Black Veevus PB 140 denier
- **Tail:** Black Krystal Flash
- **Wing:** Black rabbit Zonker
- **Body:** Black rayon chenille (medium)
- **Rib:** Wire, black (brassie)
- **Legs:** Black rubber (medium)

The Zirdle Bug is supposed to have originated around Bozeman, Montana, although I have never seen a name attached to the fly as the originator. I do know that it got its name for being a combination of a Zonker and Girdle Bug, both of which are exceptional flies in their own right.

While streamers are effective in the Great Smoky Mountains region, they are often very hard to fish effectively, especially in the smaller streams where your cast may be limited to 20 or 30 feet maximum distance. Having grown up eating trout and helping clean them for my father and grandfather, I have never cleaned one over 18 inches in the region that did not have either a large salamander or crayfish or both in its stomach. Knowing how many large fish feed on salamanders, anglers should not ignore this food source for big trout.

The Black Zirdle Bug, with its long rabbit Zonker tail and rubber legs, makes a pretty good salamander imitation. Every large rain event dislodges salamanders from debris along the edge of the river or creek bank. This rising water makes the trout go nuts

The abundance of black salamanders in the Smokies makes them a key nutrient source for larger trout. A Black Zirdle Bug is one of the finest black salamander imitations that an angler can have in their box.

and feed heavily on salamanders, crayfish, and other large forage that is swept up in the heavy current. During this phenomenon the trout will feed heavily as the water rises and keep feeding until it starts to recede, when they will transition to feeding on more-common nymphs and forage.

Over the years, I had played with different bunny patterns to try to mimic the salamanders. But on a trip to Montana, I was shown the Zirdle Bug by Mike Treloar. My immediate thought was, wow, that would be a great salamander pattern. Most of the Zirdle Bugs I see tied commercially are a size 6 to 12, but I like to really beef them up and fish them in a size 2 or 4. The Zirdle Bug is a great streamer that is even better when dead drifted, which makes it an excellent choice for fishing the Great Smoky Mountains where the smaller streams dictate drifting a streamer instead of stripping it. When dead drifted, the Zonker tail and rubber legs undulate with every current and twitch of the rod, making the fly look more alive in the water.

I used a very heavily weighted size 4 Zirdle Bug to win the Fly Fishing Masters tournament in 2006 on Noontootla Creek in North Georgia. As we were preparing to fish

Natural and Olive Zirdle Bugs are both good crayfish representations. Crayfish are another common meal of the larger trout of the region.

Releasing a rainbow trout that found a Black Zirdle Bug.

for the afternoon session, we were delayed by a thunderstorm that caused the stream to get a tea color and start rising. I had scouted the section of stream I had drawn and had seen two very large rainbows. Once we got the off-color water, I rerigged to a large Zirdle Bug weighted extremely heavy. I made my presentation to the first trout and the fly landed and went to the bottom, where I crawled it along until it was in eyesight of the first trout, then hopped it away from him. The fish's natural instincts took over and he inhaled the fly on the second hop. I was able to land and score a beautiful 20½-inch rainbow trout. I walked up to where I had seen the second trout and repeated the process to land a massive 26-inch rainbow. So with only 22 minutes off the two-and-a-half-hour clock, I had scored my two trout for total of 46½ inches.

Since that experience, I have fished the Zirdle Bug in countless colors and have found black, rust/olive, and natural to be my favorites. When tying the larger sizes (2 and 4) of the Zirdle Bug, I will often use a ¼-inch Zonker strip. However, I like to take my scissors and trim the Zonker so that it tapers to a point at the back, giving it more of a natural salamander shape.